Dear LGBTQ Studies Teacher,

Something really DIFFERENT to do in your LGBT class, something both the students and teacher will find exciting--that's what I am offering you here: my play "QUEERING ALEXANDER: 333 B.C."

I wrote it this summer so students can learn that there have always been people like us, that we gays have been important in history.

When your students act out this SUSPENSEFUL play in class, they will take the roles of Alexander the Great and his life partner as they fight with the Lesbian Legion and the Leathermen of Thrace--- against the Persians led by their lipstick lesbian queen and her transexual ally. At the end of the play both sides embrace toleration in a gorgeous INCLUSIVE WEDDING that celebrates that there are many different ways to be gay and all are ok.

The play takes about 3 hours of class time. Copies of it are available at Lulu.com

The stage directions are so complete that it will be easy for a teacher to do in class. It naturally generates rich discussion and paper topics. I have included several assessments for you to use if you wish. In addition, my partner and I would like to come to your campus for two days to help you get started--at NO COST to you. It sounds egotistical to say, but both of us are (retired) crowd pleasers, who can't wait to get back in the classroom!

You can reach us at 760-992-7491 or e-mail us at actingouthistory@gmail.com

I DEDICATE THIS PLAY TO MY HERO, LOUIS ARTHUR
ARMENTROUT, THE BEST MAN I HAVE EVER KNOWN. I AM SO
BLESSED TO BE MARRIED TO HIM!

"QUEERING ALEXANDER: LGBT 333 B.C."

A PLAY BY MICHAEL WELCH

TABLE OF CONTENTS

PREFACE

I wrote this play as a exciting, new learning activity for a college course in Queer/LGBT Studies.

It's like the plays I wrote for my book <u>CLASSROOM PLAYS for an ETHICAL WORLD</u> (which includes "THE REAL DRACULA", and "JAGUAR ATTACKS: A MAYA MYSTERY".) I designed them as a different way to teach; most of my students found this way worked well for them.

There are several reasons for this I think. One is the fact that doing a play in class, as mine are best done, is a SOCIAL learning event: it's something students DO, and do TOGETHER. Students also have told me my plays are "fun" and "real". They have fast action plots, lots of suspense, and they deal with people who have some of the feelings the students have.

I think all this will work in Queer Studies even better. Most of the students will have something important in common with the characters in the play. In addition I use our ancient past to examine some issues in gay life today.

In conclusion, I wrote this play to celebrate who we were in the past, who we are now, and who I hope we may become. I hope it works for you.

IT'S HISTORICAL FICTION

This play is historical FICTION. The "true" history of Alexander is forever lost because absolutely nothing that was written about him was written in his lifetime. Most of the important early writers wrote HUNDREDS of years after his death. The early writers agree about some things and disagree about others, and each author has his own opinion of course. Later writers are much the same---many, many different opinions about almost everything.

And very few of these writers mentioned sex; most of them totally ignored Alexander's sexuality. It is widely accepted that Alexander was married to two women and probably had at least one child, so I think we can assume he was bi-sexual.

His homosexuality is inferred from his life-long relationship with Hephaiston. That they were more than best friends is inferred from Alexander's behavior when Hephaiston died: he gave him the biggest funeral ever, and had him worshipped as a god. Also dear Mary Renault says he was! Her books FIRE FROM HEAVEN and THE PERSIAN BOY are among the best ever written about him in my opinion. They are well-researched and they're deeply moving. She too wrote historical fiction, but she was a genius, and I'm just a teacher. Please do yourself a favor and read Mary Renault.

ITS LANGUAGE IS INFORMAL

About the language of this play, I used an informal modern American style that I hope will flow naturally from the mouths of today's students. Since they have to say their parts without a prior reading, I think it was necessary for me to make the dialogue easy to read. In addition I use modern words like "gay" and "lesbian" that would not have had equivalents in ancient languages.

HOW TO USE IT IN CLASS

The easiest way to use the play is to pass out parts and then have the students read aloud from their seats. The teacher can read the stage directions out loud to make clear what actions the characters are taking.

A better way I think is to perform the play in the classroom. To do this, the teacher will have to arrange for a space in front large enough for 8 or so students to move around. This will be the stage. The students who are not in the scene will stay in their usual seats.

The teacher will probably have to gently encourage the students to do what the stage directions say to do. The stage directions tell exactly what the student/ actor should do and how they should say their parts. The teacher should be sensitive to the student's level of comfort and be careful not to push too hard. This is not a theater class!

How the parts are assigned is crucial because each student cares most about what part she/he has. The teacher may simply assign the parts as the director. This could be an interesting way to get a student to experience what it's like to be a person very different from who she/he is. If males are given female parts, I've found it's important to ask them NOT to use "feminine" voices so it doesn't get silly.

Of course the teacher can allow each student to pick the part they want. To make this time-consuming process go as fast as possible, I've found it useful to write the characters on a paper posted on a wall. When a student picks a part, their name goes on the paper by the character they pick, so the next student can see that part is taken and so he/she can take a part that's still open. This paper up in the room is important because students often forget what role they have picked. New parts need to be picked with each new scene,although the main characters can stay the same.

However the parts are picked, the teacher should be very sensitive to the feelings of the students. This play has some speeches that might make some students uncomfortable. Please don't push anyone into anything they seem uncomfortable doing, but you know that of course.

I hope the teacher also will show a SENSE OF HUMOR throughout the play. Although the play is "heavy", full of love and death, it's also a fun-to-do MELODRAMA, often intentionally extreme. I love to paint in vivid colors! I don't mind at all if the students laugh and have fun as they do this is class. After all, it's PLAY, and they're young people. The really serious parts of the play will create their own atmosphere, and in any case the main ideas of the play will come through, or at least I hope they will.

A SUMMARY OF WELCH'S QUEERING ALEXANDER

This classroom play references the superhero, action films that most young people like. It shows different ways of being gay as they might have been in the time of Alexander the Great---"LGBT 333 B.C." It centers on the love of Alexander and his Hephaiston, as a model for a successful long term relationship. It asks that we all be open-minded about the wide variety of sexuality, then and now.

It begins in the military camp of Alexander's army. A group of big, bearded soldiers talk about the wives they left behind and the men they've found to take their place. Discussing the Sacred Band of Thebes, they determine that love for each other makes them better soldiers. When the rest go to bed, two stay up to plot the murder of Alexander, who they feel must be killed soon or his relentless conquests will lead them all to death. They let in a Persian spy who wants to put poison into Alexander's morning bread.

In the next scene, Hephaiston says,"I want you to make time stand still, Alexander. I want it to be NOW forever." The King replies,"We'll always be together. OUR LOVE WILL CONQUER TIME!" They talk about the reasons for the success of their long term relationship, deciding that a commitment to mutual respect and to compromise have helped sustain their love. Hephaiston then blurts out, "Then why do you have sex with that sissy Persian Boy?", introducing both the major conflict of the play and also its theme that discrimination against feminine men is wrong.

The next scene is with the Leathermen of Thrace, mercenary soldiers who are driving their chariots to join Alexander. These men divide themselves into tops (who do the fighting from the chariot) and bottoms (who drive it.) When a bully tries to force himself on an unwilling bottom, their leader, the Stallion, intervenes, saying that their leather code demands that a person pick his own role.

In a new scene, Alexander has a breakfast meeting with his staff to plan the coming battle. The Persian Boy brings in a child to taste Alexander's food, thus saving him from the poison mentioned earlier. After this, they plan their strategy. Alexander says he's relying on the LESBIAN LEGION to surprise the Persians.

Alexander and Hephaiston decide to ride out to explore the mountains near where the battle will be fought.

In those mountains a day later, we see a happy lesbian couple who have left their abusive husbands. One has a son who regards them both as his moms. He has just returned from hunting in a hidden pass in the mountains that usually is covered with ice but now is not. All of a sudden one of the abusive husbands, enters demanding "his woman". As this gay family is getting ready to fight for its life, up ride Alexander and Hephaiston, who make the husband go away. When Alexander asks about an open pass, the son happily explains the one he's just discovered, which pleases Alexander of course.

Next we meet a transexual and two "lipstick lesbians" who are at the Persian military camp. King Darius, who wants to try a new religion, talks to Transgendered Priest, who discusses his belief that some people need to switch their sex. He thinks that sexuality is a long continuum from totally masculine to totally feminine, with many blends in between. He maintains that most people can be fine wherever they are if they just do what feels right to them and if others don't judge them. Only a few want to completely change gender, but if they do that's fine, he concludes.

King Darius finds this interesting, but he really just wants to get Transgender Priest to be his spy in the women's quarters. The Priest is ordered to find out if Darius's Royal Twin and his mother are planning to murder him.

In the woman's area Royal Twin, who's a "lipstick lesbian", argues with her ex-girlfriend about art, then she convinces her mother, Queen Sisygambis, to agree to the murder. General Memnon joins the plot.

Transgendered Priest brings Darius to the plotters. Darius exiles his sister but lets his mother alone. Darius then has a military staff meeting in which he tells his generals that they should use their huge superiority in numbers to wear out Alexander's army, then at the last send in their two secret weapons.

Elsewhere but at the same time, a regiment of women warriors find a new recruit in the powerful Lionguard. She's never had sex at all so she's surprised but pleased with the Lesbian Legion. She finds out they were started in the distant past by the poet Sappho as a way for women who didn't want a family to make a living as mercenaries. They ride horses and use bows and arrows to maximize their gender strengths.

Their queen more or less forces herself on Lionguard, which Lydia, the young second in command, finds distasteful. For this and because the queen discriminated against "fems", Lydia leads a non-violent revolution, thus becoming the new queen. She leads them off to join Alexander's forces to show the world what women warriors can do.

Several days later the battle finally takes place. After several gains and losses, Alexander is close to defeat because of the Persian elephants, but the Lesbian Legion shows up just in time since they used the secret pass through the mountains that the mountain boy told them about. They attack from the Persian rear. Seeing this, King Darius runs away, then so do his men.

Alexander and Hephaiston are furious that he gets away. When they go to the Persian camp, they meet Darius's old mother, Queen Sisygambis, who likes Alexander at once.

When they leave her, they go visit the battle field.

Seeing all the suffering, Alexander moans,"I've made this place a red landscape of Hell. It's all my fault." Hephaiston agrees with him that they should give up war and try to excel in peaceful deeds instead.

The next scene takes place in fabled Babylon, now his capital city. Alexander, Queen Sisygambis, and the Persian Boy are planning ways to peacefully join the Persians and the Greeks. They decide a big wedding may help. At this wedding, the top Greek officers will marry the royal girls of Persia. The Persian Boy suggests that to further carry out the theme of mutual acceptance, a couple from each of the homosexual groups should be invited to marry, just as the heterosexuals are. Alexander likes the idea very much.

Hephaiston enters. Seeing Persian Boy working with Alexander makes him jealous. When Alexander says the Boy is part of their team now, Hephaiston yells, "That sissy boy is no part of me."

Hephaiston, Alexander, and the Persian Boy then go to a drinking party given by their old friends, the generals of the army. One of them insults the Persian Boy. Alexander says,"Shut up or you die!" He yells back,"No, you die!" as he lunges at Alexander with a knife. Alexander has an epileptic seizure. The Persian Boy jumps in front of Alexander to take the blow, and falls dead. Hephaiston expresses one of the play's main themes as he says, "We called you "sissy boy", but we were wrong. You've proved you were more of a man than any of us."

A month later, in a magnificent palace, the INCLUSIVE WEDDING takes place with Queen Sisygambis presiding. Down the aisle march the couples: the bears, the leathermen, the leader of the Lesbian Legion and Lionguard, the mountain women, the lipstick lesbians, and the transgendered priest and his man. Then follow the Greek generals and their Persian royal girls.

Last of all come Alexander and Hephaiston with one hand on the other's shoulder and the other hand holding that of a Persian princess. At the end, Alexander says,"Our love will conquer time,I often say. I now know how. Your children and mine will grow up together, half Persian, half Greek. They'll marry each other, generation after generation. The centuries will stretch on and on. Our love will truly conquer time!"

SCENE ONE: "THE KING MUST DIE?"

Characters:

Narrator
First Soldier(of Macedon)
Second Soldier "
Third Soldier   "
Fourth Soldier "
Fifth Soldier   "
Soldier from Athens
Soldier from Thebes
Persian Spy

MARCH 19, 333 B.C.

Teacher please say: " Now I need the people playing the following parts to come up in front: First Soldier of Macedon, Second Soldier of Macedon, Third Soldier of Macedon, Fourth Soldier of Macedon, Fifth Soldier of Macedon, Soldier from Athens, Soldier from Thebes.

 All of these soldiers are sitting around a camp fire, warming their hands. Persian Spy is off stage, waiting to come on near the end. The Narrator is in front but standing somewhat apart."

NARRATOR:

Alexander is the handsome, young hero king of Macedonia, a war-like country just north of Greece. Macedonia, also called Macedon, is mostly Greek in culture at this time in history. Alexander's father, King Philip, made Macedon into a major military power, and he imposed himself as the leader of almost all the Greek city-states, including Athens.

Just before his murder, Philip was planning to attack the Persian Empire, the traditional enemy of Greece. The Persian Empire ruled a vast area from what's now Turkey all the way to India, and it included Egypt as well. This empire was much, much richer than Greece. It was ruled by Darius, the King of Kings, who commanded the world's biggest army.

As soon as Alexander became king, he invaded the Persian Empire. In a short time he fought several battles against generals sent by King Darius to keep him out. Alexander's brilliant leadership caused him to win each battle.

Now King Darius has left his capital city and has come out to personally lead his army.   He knows he must defeat Alexander or he will loose his empire. A great battle is about to begin, a battle that will decide the fate of millions of people, a battle that will change the direction of history.

We're in the camp of Alexander's men. It's March 19, 333 B.C. in the evening.   Around a dying fire sit a group of ordinary soldiers. Some of the men have a jug of cheap wine from which they drink. The men are between 20 and 45 years old, but look older because they have heavy beards. Some have grey in their short hair. Some are balding. Most have heavy, sturdy bodies. Most wear only a tunic, a short one-piece garment with no arms. They are battle-tested soldiers: strong, fit men with well-muscled, hairy arms and legs.

THIRD SOLDIER:
(He looks down as he speaks in a soft voice, almost to himself.)

I wonder if I'll be killed this time? My older brother was killed in the first battle with the Persians. He didn't last long here in Asia. Maybe there's a curse on our family. Maybe we both should have stayed back home, on our farm in Macedonia.

FOURTH SOLDIER:
(He nods his head in agreement.)

Yes, I think about that too, but I had to get away from that nagging wife of mine. All she ever did was bitch, and she never helped me much with the farm work. I worked all day, every day. Nothing but the same old endless work. At least it made me strong.
   (He flexes both of his big biceps,smiling in pride as he does it.)
I'm the strongest man here, and you men know it!

FIFTH SOLDIER:
(He feels Fourth's hard-muscled arm, then laughs. Then he makes a loud smelling noise, a sniffing sound, then laughs again.)

Yes, you're strong all right. Your SMELL is strong enough to kill a Persian all by itself!

THIRD SOLDIER:
(He speaks in a much more serious tone of voice.)

Do you men ever miss your wives?

FOURTH SOLDIER:
(He laughs so loud his big belly bounces.)

Hell, no! I was damned glad to get away from that bitch. Besides I like this one a lot better!

(He puts his arm around Fifth Soldier, who sort of tries to move away but then decides to let the arm stay around him.)

FIFTH SOLDIER:
(His expression becomes serious now.)
Well, I take care of you better than she did, from what I hear.

FOURTH SOLDIER:
You sure do. Sex with you is a lot better than it was with her. Every thing else too.

FIFTH SOLDIER:
(He holds up his jug of wine, then drinks from it.)
Damned right it is. Let's all drink to that. It takes a man to know what another man wants.

(All of the soldiers take another drink from their jugs. Some are starting to slur from the drinking.)

THIRD SOLDIER:
At least it does here in the army, where there aren't any women. We all have to help each other out, don't we?

FIRST SOLDIER:
(Joining in the conversation, he nods his head in agreement. The others pay special attention to him because he's their leader. They nod yes as he talks.)

Yes, I really think our love for men is part of what makes this army strong. We fight hard because we sleep together---hard!

THIRD SOLDIER:
(He raises his jug like a toast then drinks from it.)

I'll drink to that. Let's enjoy life as much as we can. With a big battle coming up soon, we could be dead in a few days.

SOLDIER FROM THEBES:

You Macedonians have learned much from us in the south, the real Greece. The idea you just mentioned that gay men can make the best soldiers---you got it from us. In my hometown of Thebes, we had a special unit in the army. It was called THE SACRED BAND. All the men in it were pairs of sworn lovers, sworn to die to protect their friends.

This Sacred Band was invincible for years. They fought like lions to protect their own. They won battle after battle. They became world famous.

But then came your King Philip and his young son, Alexander. Alexander and his men attacked like an enraged bull, like hundreds of enraged bulls, hundreds and hundreds. Our Sacred Band was totally out numbered. In spite of that, they fought all day to protect each other until only two were left, then they were killed. Not one man was left alive. When Alexander saw them all, lying dead in each others' arms, he cried, cried like a baby. He said, " My new army must be like them." And now it is.

SOLDIER FROM ATHENS:
(He speaks with pride in his voice, with his nose a little up in the air.)

He was wise to learn from us. Your Macedonia is a poor, wild place. We in the real Greece invented the civilization that the whole world admires so much. Especially we in Athens of course.

We even do man sex better, if you want my opinion. All you men from Macedon usually like men about your own age, and that's fine as far as it goes, and we in Athens do that too sometimes. But our best idea is to use the male sex bond for education, to keep our city the smartest in the world and tops in sports as well.

(He continues on, ignoring the obvious boredom of some of the others. His sense of superiority is all too apparent.)

As you may know, in Athens when a man reaches a certain stage in his life, when he's married and has had a son, he looks for a younger man to be his partner. He decides what thing he's best at, then he finds a younger man who's good at this too. The older one teaches the younger man how to do it better, be it philosophy or wrestling, criminal law or discus throwing. Everyone wins! The two men form a deep connection in sex and in their talent. The older one gets gratitude, the younger one gets skills. Best of all, with most of the upper class men of Athens doing this, Athens gets even better, generation by generation. No wonder we excel!

FIRST SOLDIER:
(He looks worried, frowning somewhat.)

I'm not so sure about your Athens way. What if the boy doesn't get a chance to become himself? Wouldn't an older man sometimes dominate the younger one too much?

SOLDIER FROM ATHENS:
(He smiles agreeably.)

I'm glad you're concerned for the younger one. We are too of course.

They're our sons after all! But what you're worried about is self-correcting in practice. If the older one pushes too hard, the younger one just leaves. That's the beauty of it---it's not a marriage, there are no legal strings attached. Either man can walk away if he wants to. They always have a wife or mother to take them back.

FIRST SOLDIER:
(He nods yes.)

That does make sense to me. I can easily see how good this custom is for education. No wonder Athens is so great in mind and body too. Your custom gives both men a reason to excel.

> *****************(Teacher, you might make a short written assignment at this point. You could ask the students to first explain in writing what the Soldier from Athens says about how Athens tried to use gay sex to help it excel. Then they would tell if they think this would really have worked in ancient Athens. They would next tell if they think this method would work if we tried in here and now. They would end by saying if they think it would be ok or not, to try this here.)**
> **

SECOND SOLDIER:
(He has an almost angry tone in his voice.)
Wait a minute, Athens!   There's something else about your way that bothers me. I haven't been to Athens so I've never seen how it works in your city, but I've seen what you're talking about out here in Asia, and it stinks! I've seen plenty of our soldiers going around with little sissy boys, local boys who don't even have beards. I don't like it at all. A real man shouldn't have anything to do with something so feminine---I HATE IT!

ATHENS SOLDIER:
(He puts his hand on the shoulder of Second Soldier, who shrugs it off.)

Calm down, my friend. What's it got to do with you? If one of our men gets lonely and wants some softness in his life, how does it hurt you? You like big, hairy men and he likes "feminine" guys. Why can't you get what you want, and let him be free to get what he wants? Why does it matter to you?

SECOND SOLDIER:
(He's really mad now, almost yelling. He shakes his fist at the Athens Soldier.)

Because...because... because I guess we're sort of... on the same team. (Now he looses his anger and starts to feel more scared and more sad. He puts his head down and talks in a more quiet voice.)

If some man on my team gets all girly, it worries me that I could become like that. I guess that's it.

FIRST SOLDIER:
(At first he's talking to Second Soldier, then starts to talk to everyone in the conversational group.)
I know what he means; I can't stand those sissy boys either, but we had better get used to them. Alexander himself has one now. At first I didn't believe it, but I saw them out riding together yesterday. The boy's a beauty, that's for sure. I've never seen a person of either gender have eyes like his, or hair, or a face for that matter. He's pure PERFECTION. And Alexander is crazy about him---that was clear. I think that boys like that are here to stay.

FOURTH SOLDIER:
(He yawns loudly, then drinks from his jug.)
I'm getting sleepy.

FIFTH SOLDIER:
(He laughs and puts his arm around the waist of Fourth Soldier.)
 What you mean is that you're getting horny! I see it in your tunic.

FOURTH SOLDIER:
(He lightly punches his buddy in the stomach.)
Shut up and come with me.

SOLDIER FROM ATHENS:
(He yawns, then everyone starts to yawn, some sort of faking it and rolling their eyes as they look at the couple.)
I'm getting sleepy too. Let's all go to bed, men. Most of the time the tent is more fun than the campfire, don't you think? Hey, Thebes, you look like you need a good massage. Why don't you come with me, Buddy?
(Every one goes off stage to bed except First Soldier and Second Soldier who stay behind.)

FIRST SOLDIER:
(He puts his arm around Second Soldier.)

Good night, my friends. Sleep well. We've got guard duty over at Alexander's tent so we'll see you in the morning. Don't stay UP too long!
(He laughs at his own sexual humor, but then talks in a more quiet voice to Second Soldier.)

Remember when someone tonight said he wondered if he would be killed in the battle that's coming up? You know, I've been thinking about that again too. This time we're facing a much bigger Persian army than we did last time, and the time before. One of the scouts who's been spying on them told me yesterday that he thinks they may out number us maybe TEN to one. We don't stand a chance.

SECOND SOLDIER:
That doesn't sound good, does it? And I guess their King Darius must be learning from all the battles he's lost to us so far. He must have figured out that you can always expect the unexpected from Alexander in a battle. Their king will probably be more ready this time. That's not good for us.

FIRST SOLDIER:
It's certainly not. But worse yet, if we live through this battle, there'll be another one soon, and then another and another. Do you think he'll ever stop?

SECOND SOLDIER:

I don't suppose he will. He's starting to think he's a god. He probably thinks he can't be killed.

FIRST SOLDIER:

Yes, that it. With battle after battle ,we'll eventually be killed for sure, but he thinks he can never die!

SECOND SOLDIER:

(He puts his head down in sadness.)

I want to see my home again.   I want to see my old father before he's gone. I don't want to be buried in this strange place; I want to go home.

FIRST SOLDIER:

(He now speaks louder, with confidence in his voice.)

Of course you do. That's why we have to KILL ALEXANDER! Unless he's killed, he'll get us all killed sooner or later. You know in your heart it's true!

SECOND SOLDIER:

 The first time you said that to me, I almost killed YOU as a traitor to our side. I love Alexander like we all do, but I've been thinking about what you said. I love my home more than I love him. Now you've made me see it's one or the other. Alexander must go. If we can get Alexander out of the way, our old General Parmenion will probably take over, since Alexander has no children yet. I guess we really do have to murder our King.

FIRST SOLDIER:

(He shakes hands with his friend.)

I'm glad you see that now, because tonight's the night to put our idea into effect.

SECOND SOLDIER:
(His face and voice show how shocked he is. His face soon goes from shock to fear.)

Tonight? So soon? I don't think I'm ready for this right now.

FIRST SOLDIER:
(He speaks in a firm, almost angry voice.)

Well, you have to be. In a few minutes when the moon rises, a Persian spy will come right here to us so we can secretly let him in Alexander's compound. He's a druggist. He's made some lethal poison that he'll put into the special flour that's only used to bake Alexander's bread. I paid one of the cooks to tell me about his special bread, paid him with lots of Persian gold. So the spy will put in the tasteless poison, then he'll sneak out of the cooking tent and be gone.

SECOND SOLDIER:
(He puts his head down in sadness.)

So our great hero-king will die from eating bread?

FIRST SOLDIER:
Don't think about that. Just think about how much you want to go home. This is the only way, and you know it.

SECOND SOLDIER:
I'm afraid you're right. I want to live. It's either him or me. But won't they kill us for sure, if we get caught?

FIRST SOLDIER:
But we won't get caught. The spy does the dangerous part---he might get killed---but why would someone think we had anything to do with it? There are 30 guards on duty tonight. Why would anyone single us out to blame?

(The Persian Spy sneaks in silently, dressed like a Greek, and comes up to First Soldier.)

PERSIAN SPY:

I was told to meet you here by the old oak tree. You're the man, aren't you? "The sun is about to dim."

FIRST SOLDIER:

 Yes, that's the secret pass word. And I answer, "Let's help the moon shine bright again."

PERSIAN SPY:

Obviously you're the right man. I've got the poison hidden in my sandal. Which one is the cook's tent?

FIRST SOLDIER:

(He points to the right.)
That's it. Now go do it fast. We don't want anyone to see us together.

PERSIAN SPY:

(He sneaks off silently.)
Thank you and goodbye.

FIRST SOLDIER:

(He puts an arm around his friend.)

Let's act like we're on the job now.
(Both of them stand at attention, since they're on guard duty.)
Remember---THIS NEVER HAPPENED. We'll never speak of it again.

SCENE TWO ------"OUR LOVE WILL CONQUER TIME."

MARCH 20, 333 B.C.

CHARACTERS:
NARRATOR
ALEXANDER
HEPHAISTON

NARRATOR:

It's the next day---very early morning. Alexander the King and his best friend Hephaiston are sleeping together on a soldier's bed. Their tent is small, just like his soldiers', and they sleep on the ground.

They're both in their early twenties. Hephaiston is rather tall with the build of a basketball player---long and lean. He also has a basketball player's big hands and feet. His long nose and high cheek bones give him an aristocratic look. His hair is light brown, worn rather short. He's eyes are a gentle brown with flexes of gold.

Alexander is slightly shorter and much more strongly built. He's broad shouldered with a strong chest and massive arms and legs. He's one of the best looking men that's ever lived! His hair is like a lion's mane --- dark blond and bright mixed together in a thick cascade that flows around his face. His eyes are a radiant blue-gray, like a mountain lake. He looks at those he likes (and hates) with deep, sincere attention. He holds his head a little to the right as he listens. He's as intense as the sun itself.

HEPHAISTON:
(Both men sleep naked. He suddenly sits up in bed, then looks closely into Alexander's sleeping face. He tries not to bother him, but has to so he puts his hand on the King's shoulder to wake him up.)

Alexander, I want you to make TIME stand still. I want it to be NOW forever. You could be killed today. I can't be without you!

ALEXANDER:
(He wakes up immediately, instantly alert. He sits up, then puts his arms tightly around Hephaiston. He speaks in a very serious tone, full of confidence. His voice is high but manly, with a beautiful resonance all his own.)

We'll ALWAYS be together, my friend. Our love will CONQUER time!

HEPHAISTON:
It will, won't it? Our love will conquer time!
It's just that I was having a bad dream. I dreamed someone tried to kill you. I could see you covered in blood.

ALEXANDER:
(Now he speaks in a lighter, much less serious tone.)

You're just hung-over! You always have bad dreams when you get drunk, and last night you were ROARING drunk! Remember how you tried to break up that fight, but fell down yourself, because you were laughing so hard?

HEPHAISTON:
(He's in a good mood now too, exchanging last night's drinking stories with his buddy.)

Didn't those two boys look dumb? They were trying so hard to be fierce!

ALEXANDER:
(He looks more serious again.)
Forget them. I want to tell you about a dream I had, a really vivid dream.

HEPHAISTON:
(He changes his mood instantly, to match Alexander's.)
Was it a good dream?

ALEXANDER:
(He smiles broadly and pats Hephaiston on the back.)
That's for sure! It was all about sex. It was like a play: first one scene, then another, then another. I'm afraid it'll be rather long in the telling.

HEPHAISTON:
(He takes Alexander's hand in his.)
Tell me all about it. You know I want to know everything about you.

ALEXANDER:
(He shuts his eyes to remember better.)

Well, it started when I was little.   Mother was telling me what a king has to be.   I had to be the best in everything I did. I tried day and night to please her, but my best was never good enough. She always wanted MORE from me. "You're the son of Zeus," I heard her say--- over and over. "You've GOT to do better than that."

Then in the next part of the dream, I was about ten; I was starting to get hard-ons. A servant girl saw this so she pulled out my cock and played with it. I liked it a lot. Soon I was rubbing it against her sex, which felt even better. Then my mother caught us naked. She said,"Put your tunic on, you silly boy. There'll be time for girls later,when you need a son of your own. Right now you've got to learn to throw that discus. Get to work, Son!"

The dream had these little scenes, like a play I guess, but not so formal. Just all these short little scenes. I think the next one was when I was twelve. Yes, I remember now. It was the night after my twelfth birthday party, when I got my first horse. Anyway, I was rough housing with two friends just before bed. We were wrestling naked.

Then I got a hard on when I was on top of Ptolemy. He laughed and pushed me off. But I liked it, so I pinned Cleitus fast, then rubbed my cock on him. He flipped me over and did the same to me. You can imagine the rest. From then on, we did it together a lot. It hit the spot: it just felt RIGHT. You remember that feeling, don't you?

HEPHAISTON:

(He nods his head "yes".)

I sure do. I had sex with girls until I was fifteen, then my cousin sort of made me have sex with him in a barn. It was so much better than with girls. From then on I had sex with almost every boy I knew. It was really fun and I learned a lot! Lucky there weren't any diseases then.

ALEXANDER:

(He pats his friend on the back.)

 Yes, weren't those good times! All that sex! We were all so full of teenage energy, that we did it every chance we got! It was even better than sports, wasn't it?

HEPHAISTON:

(He laughs his jolly laugh, remembering those days.)

A LOT better! And the stronger we got, the better it got: all those hard new muscles!

ALEXANDER:

(His face changes to more serious now.)

Back to my dream. The next scene I remember was the day I first had sex with YOU. You were new at my gymnasium. I noticed your warm eyes from across the floor, then I heard your jolly laugh. You weren't exactly my type, but after we talked all evening, I could see you were what I NEEDED. After we went to bed, I knew we were MADE for each other. "We fit together flowing, like a river over rocks going." Remember when I said that to you, because we were wet with sweat all night?

HEPHAISTON:

(He smiles a big smile, then hugs Alexander.)

Of course I remember. It was the beginning of my life, at least the happy part.

ALEXANDER:
(Alexander gets a glowing look in his eyes, like he's seeing a vision.)

And it's still that way for us, isn't it? You're the center of the world to me. NOTHING is real until I share it with you.
(Now his face becomes more thoughtful.)

Why do you think we've done so well? Most couples, straight or gay, fight most of the time, don't they? Look at my mother and father; they fought like wildcats every time they were together. I think she may have had him killed. I wouldn't put it past her.

HEPHAISTON:
They really hated each other. Anyone could see that. Most couples aren't that bad, but many aren't very good either, are they? Most of the young couples we know only last a few months at most. They start to be unfaithful almost as soon as they first get together. Why is that, do you think?

ALEXANDER:
I think the straight people often don't really have much in common. They just run out of things to talk about, unless they have children, and that causes problems too. We gay people have a lot more in common with our mates, but when you get two men together you also have twice the promiscuous energy, so that leads to trouble most of the time.

HEPHAISTON:
 But why have we done better?

ALEXANDER:
Part of it's only luck I think. We happened to have found the right person at the right time, and we happen to both have a big talent for friendship. But a lot of it is how hard we work at it too. I think we both always try to be really nice to each other, day in and day out. We have a COMMITMENT to kindness and mutual respect.

HEPHAISTON:

That's really true, isn't it? We're committed to be nice to each other ALL the time, not just when we're in a good mood. I've noticed most couples quit doing that after a few weeks.

ALEXANDER:

And also we have rules that we've worked out together. We don't just do what we feel like. We do what we've promised to each other. We both look at handsome men, but we've agreed to let each other do that. We don't give in to little jealousies. We're secure enough to let our partners have their own friends, but we always put each other first. We're faithful where it counts.

HEPHAISTON:

(He suddenly RAISES HIS VOICE, almost shouting.)

Then WHY do you have sex with that nelly Persian Boy?

ALEXANDER:

(He talks in a calm, controlled way, in a normal voice, not mad at all.)

I've been waiting for you to bring that up. This is painful, isn't it? It's hard to talk about. We don't want to upset the good life we have together, but we need to talk this out now I know. Please don't start to cry.

HEPHAISTON:

(He is starting to cry but is trying to control it.)

I can't help it. That little slut is going to wreck everything we have. I HATE his girly guts!

ALEXANDER:

(He frowns deeply as he tries hard to be both honest and kind; he's trying to figure this out for the first time.)

Why do I have sex with him? I guess part of it is just variety. We've been together for a long time. Every thing is new with him. But it's better with YOU, it really is. Every time I'm with him, I think afterwards, it would have been better with you. Our sex is the best.

So I think it's not mostly about sexual variety, but more some other thing entirely. I think it's connected with him being a former lover of the Persian King of Kings; it almost has to be. Several weeks ago when he got away from King Darius and came here to me, I guess it made me feel that I must be better than the Persian King. I mean I think I AM better, but here was living proof of it: his boy wanted ME instead. No matter that Darius had abused the boy; what mattered was the boy chose me instead. I won.

HEPHAISTON:
(He's trying hard to see things from Alexander's viewpoint.)

Yes, and he's a STUNNING beauty, that's for sure--- those big, black soulful eyes. He's too soft for me, more girl than boy, but I can see why you fell for him.

ALEXANDER:
There's more to it too I think. His being a PERSIAN makes it all work for me. When I get inside him, it's like I'm getting inside this strange new country that I want to rule. His BODY is like all Persia in some crazy, magic way. When I fill him with myself, it's like I'm taking over the whole Persian Empire. I can't explain it any better to you, but I feel it's deeply true. I NEED him, don't you see? Not like I need you--- for myself--- but I need him as a KING.

HEPHAISTON:
(He slowly nods his head up and down to show he understands, then he raises his right arm with his index finger pointing up, like a preacher emphasizing an important idea. He speaks in a very serious tone, and makes a rather long pause between each sentence.)

Then you must have him. You must fulfill your destiny. YOU must rule the world.

ALEXANDER:

(He slowly shakes hands with his partner, to show they have reached an agreement.)

Good, then we've reached an agreement, a compromise we both can live with. It's like we always do; we try to meet each other's needs as best we can. I give you the promise that our love will conquer time, and you give me the Persian Boy for now. We're ONE again.

HEPHAISTON:

(His face shows his relief that they're ok now. He's glad to get back to everyday concerns.)

That's what I need to live. Now let's get dressed, my friend. We have to be at the staff meeting by sunrise. All the leaders of the army will be waiting for you.

ALEXANDER:

(He smiles broadly, also glad to be back to work. They put on tunics, with a white toga like thing over them. They put on simple sandals.)

Yes, we have to make our battle plan. If ONLY I had the mobile force I need. Our foot soldiers are the best, but I also need a force that can move fast. The Lesbian queen said she'd bring her horse-mounted archer army, but there's been no sign of them yet.

HEPHAISTON:

Yes, that's true, but we heard last night that the horse soldiers of Thrace will be here today or tomorrow at the latest. The Stallion himself is leading the Leathermen---that's what the messenger said.

ALEXANDER:

Thank Zeus for that! Their horsemen will give me the speed I need. I hope they get here soon!

*********** DEAR TEACHER, THIS WOULD BE A GOOD PLACE TO ASK THE STUDENTS TO WRITE A SHORT PAPER. IT COULD BE LIKE THIS.

Please write your answers to these questions in order and using only full sentences:

FIRST PARAGRAPH

1. What's one of the reasons Alexander and Hephaiston have had such a good, long-lasting relationship?
2. What's a second reason?
3. What's a third reason?

SECOND PARAGRAPH

4. What big problem do they have in their relationship?
5. How does it make Hephaiston feel?
6. How do they deal with it?

THIRD PARAGRAPH

7. Do you want to have a good, long-lasting relationship in your life, at least eventually?
8. What could you learn for your future relationship, from the reasons for their success Alexander and Hephaiston talk about? (Several sentences might be needed here.)
9. Your relationship will develop problems for sure. They ALWAYS do! What could you learn about problem solving in your relationship from the way Alexander and Hephaiston handle their problem?

SCENE THREE---- " THE LEATHER MEN OF THRACE"

MARCH 18, 333 B.C.

CHARACTERS:
NARRATOR
JASON
HECTOR
BULLY
THE STALLION
FIRST GUARD
SECOND GUARD

NARRATOR:
It's early in the morning two days before the last scene. The Leathermen of Thrace are twenty miles from Alexander. They are on their
way to join up with him. Their large camp takes up most of a small
valley. Big, beautiful horses, several thousand of them, graze in the
new spring grass. There are about 200 chariots carefully lined up in
rows inside a fence of leather cords, just what Alexander needs for a
mobile force.

Everything you see is made of leather: the tents, the horse
equipment,and the clothing of the men. Because it's still cold, most
have on jackets with many silver studs attached.

The thousand men range in age from fifteen to forty. Almost all are
very, very big---both tall and packed with muscle. They have shaved
heads and short, dark beards. When they take off their leather
jackets, you can see that most of them have tattoos---blue tattoos,
mostly of horse's heads. Each horse stands for an enemy the man
has killed. Unlike other Greeks, they all wear tall, black boots.

Teacher, please say, " I need the following people in our stage area:

JASON and HECTOR. BULLY is just off stage, ready to enter. THE STALLION and FIRST GUARD and SECOND GUARD are on the other side, ready to come in a bit later."

JASON:
(He yells this.)
Because the STALLION told us to, that's why!

HECTOR:
(His face shows he feels shocked at being yelled at by his boyfriend, but he adjusts to that fast and starts to nod in agreement.)

Yes, he's our Phallic King. I know that for sure. I've felt his power inside me several times this month. Our Thracian Horse God put him in charge. We have to obey his every word. That's what my father taught me.
(He now starts to frown deeply.)
    But still I don't want to wrestle naked today. I'm sick of always losing. No matter who I have to wrestle, I always end up on the bottom. It's fine sometimes, but I never get to be the top.

JASON:
(He puts his hand on Hector' shoulder, and uses a sympathetic voice.)

That's tough for you I know. That's why you're not good at throwing spears from a chariot; you don't get enough practice, do you? As the bottom, you always have to handle the horses, so you hardly ever get to be the man who stands in the chariot and throws the spears.
The top's the one who kills the enemy, so he gets all the glory.

HECTOR:
You're right about that. When the army recruiter came to our village, he never mentioned that. He made me think all the men get glory. I wanted to feel like a man; that's why I joined up.

JASON:
That's what they always talk about, isn't it? Being a real man! They come into our villages. They tell the teenage boys that real men fight

and have sex with with other men. They say the boys who like girls should just stay in the village, marry the neighbor girl, and farm the rest of their lives.

HECTOR:

Yea, I wasn't very interested in girls---not like some of my friends---so I joined up. They said they'd make me a man.

JASON:
(He puts an arm around his friend.)

Hector, you ARE a man! Remember how you won the race last week? You're the fastest young man in our group, and everyone knows it. Plus look at how you excel in writing war poems. The STALLION himself said an army needs good word-men like you, to keep our spirits up.

HECTOR:
(He puts his head down in shame.)
Then why do they call me "Loser", and tease me all the time?

JASON:
Because they don't KNOW you, don't know who you really are. You're a real man, that's for sure, but maybe your style of manhood would fit in better somewhere else. Like in Athens or, come to think of it, in ALEXANDER'S ARMY. Everybody says Alexander's smart and full of new ideas. He'd value who you are, I'll bet.

HECTOR:
(He gives his friend a kiss on the cheek.)

Thank you very much, my friend. You've made me feel better. Maybe I should quit trying to be this kind of man. Maybe Alexander's type is closer to what I am inside. I think I'll try his style soon.

JASON:
I really think you should. This brotherhood of Leathermen is based

on POWER after all. You never have cared much about that. The men here worship aggressive maleness; that's not your style. These men are all about masculine power. They feel their manhood most, when they are dominating other strong men. They want to overcome each other to prove they're the better man. That's just what they're like, and that's fine as long as they don't hurt anyone.

But that's just not you. You don't like too much competition. You don't want to be the boss or the slave. You just want to be yourself.

HECTOR:
That's it, isn't it? I need to be who I am. It doesn't matter what other people say a man should be. I know I must be ME.

(Hearing a noise, he looks behind himself, then frowns.)
But for now, here comes trouble! I guess I'll have to wrestle one more time.
(Bully enters. He comes up to Hector and Jason. He has a mean expression on his face.)

BULLY:
(He grabs Hector by the shoulders and yells right in his face.)

Damned right, you have to wrestle, Bottom Boy, and you're going to wrestle me. The Stallion told me I could pick my opponent so I pick YOU!

JASON:
(His face shows that he's really mad. He speaks in a loud voice to Bully, who turns his head to hear who's talking.)

You pile of shit! That's against the Horse God's rules. You know the rules say the match ups have to be random. Not even the Stallion can change that. And you know I'm right!

BULLY:
(He takes his hands off of Hector, then uses his right to throw a fast punch into Jason's belly. The unexpected blow knocks the wind out of Jason who falls to the ground.)

I know you're DOWN, that's what I know. Now let me have my bottom boy!
(Bully grabs Hector by neck and pulls him off towards the left.
Jason, on the ground,gets up quietly, then moves fast to Bully.)

JASON:
(He yells a sort of war-hoop scream and tackles Bully from behind, which makes Bully fall down hard.)

Ya Hoo! Ya Hoo!
Now you're down, Asshole! Why don't you LICK my boots!

(Bully jumps up and grabs Jason like a bear, with both arms around him.)

BULLY:
I've got you, Girl! I'm twice the man you are!

(Bully, who is a lot bigger than Jason, lets Jason go a moment. Jason pulls back a foot or two, then Bully kicks Jason in the groin hard with his knee, so Jason goes down again. Then Bully goes to Hector and grabs him by the neck and starts to choke him. He commands Hector....)

Come to Daddy, Boy! The Stallion said I could pick who I want to wrestle and I want you, Sweetheart!(He starts to kiss him.)

(Just then from the rear up comes the Stallion, a mighty man who is obviously much stronger than Bully, and he also is their leader of course.)

THE STALLION:
(His handsome face looks angry, and his voice are full of menace.)

You goddamn LIER! Don't you put words in my mouth.
(The Stallion slugs Bully in the jaw hard, so Bully goes down.)

I said NO SUCH THING. The wrestling pairs must be chosen randomly, by lot. Not even I can change that law. We have it straight from the Horse God himself.

Not that I'd do anything to help you anyway. I've been hearing reports every day about how you take advantage of the new men. This time I've caught you in the act.

You son of a bitch, you've broken our Leathermen Code of Honor. You could make us all look weak and girly. We Leathermen fight rough---that's why other men look up to us. But we fight FAIR as well. We always fight like REAL men, not like mean boys. You've disgraced us all, you stupid shit!

For this I'm going to punish you like you deserve. You're going to find out how it feels to be a bottom!

(He turns to talk to two of his giant guards who were following just behind him.)

Guards, take this weakling over to that tree and tie him there naked. I want to see his butt.

FIRST GUARD:
Yes, Sir. I'll rip his tunic off right now!
(He tears it off roughly.)

SECOND GUARD:
(He sort of whispers to his buddy.)

Doesn't he have a nice little ass!
(The Stallion winks at the two guards, then he turns to talk to Jason and Hector.)

THE STALLION:
You there, the one he wanted for his boy, you come over here and slap him first. Slap him hard on his bare butt; slap him until his butt 's red, then you, his friend, you beat his butt, then all you men over there. Keep it up until I say stop.

We'll teach him a lesson he'll never forget: in this man's army, you obey the rules, or all hell will fall on you.

JASON:
(He goes up to the Stallion, a brave thing to do, and taps him on the shoulder.)

Sir, may I bother you for a moment please? The man the bully picked on, Sir.....

THE STALLION:
Yes, go on, Son.

JASON:
He can WRITE, sir!   He even can write poetry, like Sappho or like the great Homer who wrote the "Iliad", you remember--- about all those ancient soldiers, men like you?

THE STALLION:
He can write, yes, that's good, but what do you want from me?

JASON:
I want you to put him on your headquarters staff, where he can use his education to help you keep track of all the work you do.

THE STALLION
(He pats him on the back.)

That's a GREAT idea. I have a hell of a lot to do. I keep all of it in my head, but sometimes I forget. He can write it down! If I'm going make it as a general in ALEXANDER'S army, I'll need all the help I can get.

(The Stallion really looks at Hector now. His face shows that he likes what he sees! He smiles a big smile, winks at the boy, and puts his arm around Hector.)

You're a very handsome boy. I can think of SEVERAL things you can do for me.

(Loud noises are heard of a horse approaching fast.)

There's the great Alexander's messenger right now. His army must be near. We'll join them by tomorrow morning. A big battle is coming soon. I can almost smell the blood!

SCENE FOUR---------"WAR PLANS"

MARCH 20, 333 B.C.

CHARACTERS:

BLACK CLEITUS
PARMENION
PTOLEMY
WHITE CLEITUS
THE STALLION
PERSIAN BOY
ALEXANDER
HEPHAISTON
TASTER
NARRATOR

> Teacher, please say, " I need the following up here in our stage area: BLACK CLEITUS, PARMENION, PTOLEMY, WHITE CLEITUS, THE STALLION, NARRATOR, PERSIAN BOY. ALEXANDER and HEPHAISTON are off stage. THE STALLION is off stage. TASTER is off stage also. The NARRATOR stands off alone."

NARRATOR:
It's early the day before the big battle. Alexander's top officers are having a staff meeting. They're sitting around a table in a large but very simply furnished tent.

BLACK CLEITUS:

A POISON boy? Who the hell says Alexander needs a boy to taste his food? He's our hero. We're the toughest men on earth, and we love him. Who would want to kill him?

PARMENION:

Besides that, we're Macedonians; we STAB our kings. I was right next to King Philip when the traitor stabbed him with a sword. I helped catch and kill that stupid kid, with a SWORD too, of course.

PTOLEMY:

Yes, poison sounds so PERSIAN, doesn't it? Those Persians would do that sort of thing. They're sneaky and sly, like one of their cats. Didn't their King Darius poison both his brothers so he could take the throne?

PARMENION:

I remember something like that. They do so many cowardly things, I get them all mixed up. Now that I think of it, he poisoned his father too. How bad is that? Aristotle is right when he says they should be ruled by us. They're just GIRLS really. Look at all those clothes they wear, those stupid pants. Real men go nearly naked, don't they? Real men dress like us!

BLACK CLEITUS:

Speaking of Persian girls, here comes the worst one now. Look at the fancy scarf around his neck, and all those pearls. He even wears EYE MAKE UP! God damn him!

PARMENION:

These feminine boys make me sick! It's bad enough that half the army's gay, and worse that the King is too, but at least those men sound and act like men. That Persian Boy's voice is way too high, and he's too graceful for a man. I HATE him!

THE STALLION:

(He is talking mostly to himself.)
I think he's beautiful. I've never had one like that.

WHITE CLEITUS:
He's not my type, but he's good looking, that's for sure.

PTOLEMY:
I'd keep my voice down, if I were you. He belongs to Alexander, and he seems to like the boy quite a bit.

PARMENION:
I know that, and I HATE it. He's turning into a goddam Persian! No wonder he's pulling away from me and all his older generals, all of us who worked for his father. He knows his father would be ashamed of him. Going all Persian on us! He's letting the whole army down.

NARRATOR:
The Persian Boy looks like a pearl: he has a glorious, gentle glow. Like a pearl, he looks soft, but has real strength inside. He has long, full hair, rather like Alexander's, but his hair is raven black.
He has a perfect nose and sculptured lips that look made for love, but it's his long-lashed eyes that glow the most. They're like the night sky, both dark and bright. They're deep black pools of love.

PERSIAN BOY:
(He's carrying several fancy pillows and is holding a bouquet of red tulips.)

Don't mind me, gentlemen. Please go on with your work. I just want to make this place more worthy of Alexander.

(He puts the flowers in a vase and puts the pillows in several places on the floor, one quite near Parmenion.)

I think I'll put one here.
PARMENION:
(His face looks really mad.)

Don't you get near me, Boy. You smell like a whore, and you're wearing MAKE UP, for gods' sake!
(He slaps Persian Boy in the face, hard. The boy doesn't look too surprised.)

PERSIAN BOY:
(He speaks in a calm, polite, rather high pitched voice, rather like that of Curt from "Glee".)

I'm sorry I've offended you, Sir. About the make up, in the court of the Persian King, where I was until recently, make-up for men is REQUIRED. King Darius commanded it. Painted eyes have long been a part of formal court clothes. Some people think it's because when the court is outdoors in the bright sun, the make-up seems to lessen the glare of the sun.

PARMENION:
(He makes a fist at Persian Boy and screams at him.)

Well you're NOT in a Persian court, you fool. We're all FREE Macedonians and Greeks here. No Persian shit for us!

PERSIAN BOY:
(He's discouraged so he looks down and speaks in a rather soft voice.)

I was supposed to teach you men how to make the total PROSTRATION bow like we Persians do to our King of Kings. Alexander told me he would like it if you gentlemen learned to do it, so the Persians here don't feel so odd when only they know how to honor Alexander properly.

PARMENION:
(He's now so mad he's close to a heart attack.)

YOU teach ME? You teach me how to crawl on the floor to Alexander? I wiped his nose when he was a boy. I taught him how to swim!

BLACK CLEITUS:
The make-up issue is rather silly when you think about it. Who cares what you put around your eyes? But the business about prostration really matter to me.

I see us as fighting for the GREEK IDEA. To me that means that in our Greek culture, the individual really matters. It's not the group; it's each separate person that counts. To me this bowing your head to the floor for the King, this is against the GREEK IDEA. This is worshiping the GROUP. That's the Persian way. Our way is, or at least should be, that each man by himself is FREE!

PTOLEMY:

In theory I agree with you, but in practice, don't we pretty much have to do what he wants? He's our leader; he's led us this far with victory after victory. He's the greatest soldier since the world began! If he wants me to bow down to him like the Persians do, well, I'll do it. I'd do ANYTHING for him, and so would most of his men.

Since I'm said to be his illegitimate brother, I'm in charge when he's not here, so I say men, let's drop this issue for now. He'll decide when he wants to, and we'll do what he says.

NARRATOR:

Unnoticed by the military men, who continue at the table, going on with their talk, the Persian Boy leaves them, bowing silently, then he moves to the middle of the stage where he hides behind a curtain. He waits there until Alexander and Hephaiston come from the other side and enter the middle. The Persian Boy comes out from the curtain, bows low and then approaches Alexander, who smiles when he sees who it is. Hephaiston frowns and starts to walk on.

HEPHAISTON:
(He speaks with anger in his voice.)
I'll walk on since your little "friend" is here.

ALEXANDER:
(He nods in agreement and then gives his full attention to Persian Boy.)
Yes, go on and tell them I'll be there soon.

PERSIAN BOY:
(He kisses Alexander on the cheek shyly. He speaks with simple sincerity and great intensity.)

I'm sorry to bother you, Great King, but my heart is BURSTING with love. I have to see you, or I'll die.

ALEXANDER:
(He raps his arms around Persian Boy and kisses him with passion. They are locked in each other's arms, then pull their heads back just enough to talk softly to each other.)

Sweet Boy, then let me save you with a kiss. I miss you too. I've been so into war, I haven't time for love it seems.

PERSIAN BOY:
I waited in your bed last night, but you never came.

ALEXANDER:
I worked all night planning for the battle.

PERSIAN BOY:
(He takes Alexander's head in his hands as he stares into his eyes.)

Then take me now. Your cock's a thunder bolt; it lights me up inside. You really are the son of Zeus, you know. I can tell by that clean sunshine smell you always have, even when you're dirty. Only gods smell like that. All my Persian people say that's so.

ALEXANDER:
(His face takes on a special look of interest, like now he's hearing about a favorite subject.)

So you and your people think I smell like a god? Well, right now I want to show you that I make love like a god too. I NEED to be with you too, you know. You give yourself to me more than anyone else in my life. I love that! And you RELAX me, you let me slow down for a while.

I treasure you, Sweet Boy. My body is HUNGRY for yours. But we can't be together now. There's work I have to do. All these men *(He gestures with his hand all around him.)* depend on me. Their lives are in my hands.

Maybe tonight. Come to me then. If I'm still awake we'll make love, but don't wake me if I'm asleep. Zeus often comes to me in my dreams.

PERSIAN BOY:
(He bows low and then exits slowly with his body facing Alexander,as one does to royalty.)

I hear and I obey, Great King. I'll come to you tonight, hoping. Now I have to return to my servant's duty.

ALEXANDER:
(He walks fast to where the generals are siting around a table. They bow to him as he appears but not nearly so low a bow as Persian Boy has done. He looks at each of them carefully, intensely, as if he sees their souls. After a moment or two, he sits down at the table.)

Thank you for waiting, my friends. Please sit down. We have important work to do; the battle will take place soon. We need to finish our plans.

(Persian Boy and a young chap who is the Taster enter and come up to Alexander and bow, standing up, from the waist. Persian Boy looks at Alexander, waiting for permission to speak.)

HEPHAISTON:
(He puts up his right hand palm, making a "don't bother us right now" gesture. His face is frowning.)

Don't bother us right now, Boy. We have MEN'S war work to do.

PERSIAN BOY:
(He puts his head down humbly. Taster looks terrified. Persian Boy looks at Alexander, ignoring Hephaiston.)

Begging Your Majesty's pardon, don't you need your breakfast first? You know your day goes better when you've had a good breakfast.

ALEXANDER:
(He smiles warmly at Persian Boy.)

 You know me well; that's true. Yes, let's eat now. Serve us here at our seats.

PERSIAN BOY:
One more thing please, Your Majesty. You remember when I suggested that Your Majesty should have a food taster to protect you from being poisoned. I have a boy right here who will do the job, if you wish it, Great King.

ALEXANDER:
(He reaches out to shake hands with Taster, who is trembling with awe and fear.)

You're a handsome lad; you look healthy too.   What's your name, Boy? I like to know the names of the people who serve me.

TASTER:
My name is Aristotle, Sir. My father was a Greek.

ALEXANDER:
(He gives a friendly laugh.)

That was my teacher's name back home.   He helped me quite a bit.

TASTER:
(His fear gone, he smiles broadly.)

I'll help you all I can, Sir. I'd give my life for you.

ALEXANDER:
(He points to a place right next to himself.)
Thank you, Aristotle. Why don't you stand right here by me?   From now on, everything I eat or drink will be tasted first by you. I hope you don't get fat or drunk!*(He laughs a little at his own joke.)*

TASTER:
(He now feels comfortable with Alexander so he smiles.)

I'll be careful, Your Majesty. I promise!

ALEXANDER:

That's a deal, Aristotle. Now please serve the meal. Make sure I get my special kind of bread while it's hot. It's so much better that way.

PERSIAN BOY:
(He bows then leaves to get the food, which he puts on a big silver tray,then returns and approaches Alexander,smiling.)

Here's your bread, Great King---- hot, just like you ordered, Sir. But Aristotle, you must eat some first.

NARRATOR:

The Taster pulls off a small piece of the King's bread, eats it, and then immediately starts to choke and cough violently. He then grabs his throat in pain, yells loudly, then dies,falling to the ground.

HEPHAISTON:
(He jumps out of his chair, goes to Taster, knells down to take his pulse, then says....)

By Hades, he's DEAD. One taste and he's dead! I've never heard of poison that strong.

(He then turns to Alexander, stands up and hugs him tightly, then he releases him a little so he can see Alexander's face. He starts to cry a little.)

It could have been YOU, my love. You were just one moment from death. I could have LOST you.

ALEXANDER:
(He puts his arm around Hephaiston to comfort him, as he still cries softly.)
But you DIDN'T, you see. I have to win great glory before I die, and you'll be at my side, right to the very end. Nothing can block my destiny, *(he makes a long pause)* but only losing you.

BLACK CLEITUS:
(His voice is full of rage as he screams.)
Who did this thing? Who tried to kill our king?

PTOLEMY:
(He's angry too but he's keeping his calm as he tries to think it through.)

Who would WANT him dead? We all love him with our whole hearts. And who would lead us in battle, if he were dead?

PARMENION:
(He shakes both of his fists in extreme anger.)

It's the goddamn Persians; it has to be. They're trying to poison him, because they know they can't beat him fair.

WHITE CLEITUS:

The Goddamn cowards!

HEPHAISTON:
(He points his finger at Persian Boy as he speaks with deadly seriousness, then he gets out his dagger and holds it up for all to see.)

Yes, and we have the guilty Persian---right over there! He was the Persian king's boy just a few months ago. DARIUS sent him here to kill Alexander, to kill my man, to kill my one true love. I'm going to CUT his Persian throat!

ALEXANDER:
(He speaks in a dignified, calm, but firm voice.)

No, you're not, my friend. He wouldn't do that to me; I know the boy, you don't. And let's not play the Persian card. Just because he's Persian, he doesn't mean he has to be bad. Let's try to get BEYOND countries, so we can judge each man by what he is, not by WHERE he's from.

(Alexander and Hephaiston look intensely at each other for quite a while, then Alexander reaches his right hand out to Hephaiston, offering to shake hands.)

I mean this, Hephaiston, I really mean it. You HAVE to trust me on this.

HEPHAISTON:
(He still frowns but he slowly takes the hand that Alexander offers him.)

Then I do. I HAVE to. You're the king of my heart.

ALEXANDER:
(He turns around and now is talking to all the people in the room in a matter of fact, business as usual tone.)

Please take the boy's body out of here and give him a good burial at once.

(His face suddenly looks stricken; it now sinks in that someone really hates him.)

I order all of you to say NOTHING about this, or I will have you killed. This NEVER happened.
  (He almost breaks down but does not yet. He speaks in a soft but very intense voice. He's starting to shake now.)

I can't STAND that someone hated me that much.

NARRATOR:

All of a sudden, Alexander shuts his eyes and his face goes blank: he's having a sort of epileptic seizure. He doesn't move or talk for a full minute. All the other people there see this immediately, but then each looks away, as if he's seeing something he's seen before but knows he is not supposed to notice. After the minute, Alexander opens his eyes, blinks them a few times, and then goes on as if nothing has happened.

ALEXANDER:

(He acts as if he never had the seizure, totally normal.)

Gentlemen, we have work to do. Now, what's going to be our battle plan? Let's think of it as problem solving. First let's figure out the major parts of the Persian problem.

Ptolemy, please go first. What's the most important part of the problem?

PTOLEMY:

I'll try, but this new way of thinking isn't easy for me. Let's see, of course the number one problem is the SIZE of the Persian army. Our spy tells us theirs may be ten times bigger than ours.

BLACK CLEITUS:

Another problem is the geography of the place where we'll fight. We're here in the wide valley of the Snow River. The valley gets more narrow as the river runs down slowly towards the great Euphrates River, which is a long way off of course.

Tall mountains, covered in snow, wall the valley in on both sides. One of the native guides says there are several paths through the mountains, but they're so high in elevation that they're deep in snow all year. The other guide wasn't sure about the paths, but he says he's seen several glaciers in the mountains on both sides.

The geography leaves us no choice: we simply MUST come down the valley to where they are camped. Of course they'll make their army into a giant wall that will stretch from the mountains on one side all the way to the mountains on the other side. Their wall of men will be thousands of men thick. We have to attack that wall over and over, until we can break through and capture King Darius. If we can get him, their whole army will fall apart at once. We'll win.

(The Stallion comes in with a swagger. He has his arm around young Hector, his new secretary, who is holding a tablet to write on.
Both come up to Alexander and bow deeply.)

THE STALLION:

I'm very sorry I'm late, Great King. I overslept. This boy here wore me out last night! He's the BEST I've ever had!
(He laughs loudly and pats Hector on his butt.)

ALEXANDER:
(He laughs and winks at the Hector and at The Stallion.)
And that's saying something, isn't it? You've had hundreds from what I've heard.!

HEPHAISTON:

Alexander, we need to get back to planning the battle, don't you think?

ALEXANDER:
Of course we do. You're ALWAYS right, my friend!

THE STALLION:
What have you men talked about so far?

ALEXANDER:
We're doing PROBLEM SOLVING, the sort of organized thinking my teacher Aristotle often talked about. We just finished defining the problem. Now we're going to work on a SOLUTION.
(He turns to the others.)

Now, men, what's the solution? Let's put together a battle plan that will solve the Persian problem for good. Who's got an idea?

PTOLEMY:

We have to use our phalanx formations. Since our foot soldiers are organized in large, solid squares of men, each holding an 18 foot long pike, we'll ADVANCE on the enemy. With the long pikes out in front and in the air, and with our men in helmets and breast plates, the enemy will think that giant, metal hedgehogs are coming straight at them. I'll bet their front ranks will turn and run. They have so far! Most of their men aren't professional soldiers like us. Most of them are farm boys forced into the army. Yes, they'll RUN!

HEPHAISTON:

Yes, of course! Alexander's phalanx idea has caused us to win every battle we've fought so far, and we'll use most of our men in this way, but we need another Alexander SURPRISE, don't you think?

ALEXANDER:

You're right again. I have to think up another unexpected thing to catch them off guard. Now what could it be this time?

THE STALLION:

Hey men, I have a GREAT idea! Let's attack them AT NIGHT! No one ever does that. We'll catch those trouser-wearing Persians with their PANTS DOWN, quite literally!
(All the other people laugh loudly at this funny, unusual idea.)

ALEXANDER:

(He jumps up and uses his right hand and index finger to scold the Stallion. He has a deep frown on his face.)

That's a DUMB idea! That's a coward's idea. I don't want to STEAL my victory! I want to win all my victories fair and square, abiding by the rules of war.

THE STALLION:
(His face shows surprise at being yelled at, but he bows his head in submission to the King.)

It was just an idea, Great King. Forget I ever said it.

ALEXANDER:
(Alexander nods at him fast and then returns to his business as usual voice and expression, then he snaps his fingers and his face brightens up.)

The Stallion has just given me an idea! Let's have his Leathermen on their horses hide behind the forest on our battle left. We'll let the Persians attack us. We'll have our phalanxes stand steady and take the their first attack, which will probably throw them into some confusion. Then I'll lead my Companion Calvary, 400 hundred of our best men on horses---I'll have them gallup up to the Persians and start hacking away at them hard: horsemen against horsemen.

WHITE CLEITUS:
Yes,that will do it. Our calvary will just ride them down. We've done it many times.

ALEXANDER:
(He suddenly looks concerned, then happy again.)
But that's a problem,isn't it? It's exactly what they'll expect. They will send their cavalry over to try to stop ours, so they'll be on our right side. All the attention will be where I am as usual.
    Then when the trumpet blows, when most of their men are over fighting me, the Stallion will gallup out from the LEFT. They'll be so busy fighting me they may not even notice the Stallion riding up to them until it's too late. The Leathermen will smash them from behind, while I'll get them from the front. Our phalanxes will cause their foot soldiers to run away.

HEPHAISTON:
But what will happen to DARIUS? And don't forget our spy today said that Darius has his twin sister and his mother with him.

PTOLEMY:

And remember that spy said there was talk in the Persian lines, that King Darius has a SECRET WEAPON ready to use on us!

PARMENION:

Actually the spy said Darius had TWO secret weapons ready.

ALEXANDER:

Well, let's all think together. What sort of things could the secret weapons be? They might be something to throw, but we haven't seen any machines to throw so I think we can leave that out.
What else could be the secret weapon? It almost has to be some kind of weird new animal I'd say.

HEPHAISTON:

Alexander, remember when our teacher Aristotle was talking about strange animals he had heard reports of but had not seen for himself? Well, one of these lived in Arabia, as I remember, and that's not so far from here.   I think Aristotle said the animal could run really fast and it had something unusual about its back, I forget what that was.

ALEXANDER:

I do remember that! Aristotle knows more about animals and plants than any man alive; remember how he classified them into different groups?

HEPHAISTON:

What I remember was how he made us MEMORIZE all that new science !
But we need to get back to battle business, don't we?

WHITE CLEITUS:

Like what's the OTHER secret weapon? I don't like the sound of that.

PARMENION:

It's probably something ridiculous since it's the Persians. It might involve the way they worship fire. Maybe they've invented some fire weapon. I've heard about some sticky, black material that seeps from the ground down in Arabia.

PTOLEMY:
 I've heard about that too. We'd better have extra amounts of water, just in case it's that.

ALEXANDER:
That's a good idea; more water's always good after a battle in any case.

HEPHAISTON:

Alexander, you still don't look satisfied. I know your face well; that's NOT your "well,we're done" face.

ALEXANDER:
(He smiles at Hephaiston and puts his arm around him.)
You're right of course. You know me better than I know myself.
I was just thinking that I wish I had ONE MORE SURPRISE for them.
Something REALLY unexpected.

HEPHAISTON:
There's still the the LESBIAN LEGION!   Remember you paid their Queen Sappho the Tenth to bring us her regiment of mounted archers? She said she would try to get here as fast as she could, but she had another war to finish first, a war with Rhodes, I think it was.

ALEXANDER:
(He gives Hephaiston a big hug and smile.)

Yes, that's EXACTLY it! I knew I had left something out. Those Lesbians are supposed to be the best horsemen on earth.*(He laughs a little.)* I guess I should say the best horsePEOPLE on earth, shouldn't I?
They're said to be fast and dead-eye accurate with their bows and arrows. I know I can think of some great way to use them in the battle. If only they would get here SOON.

HEPHAISTON:

Before they get here, let's do one more thing: let's go do some serious scouting for ourselves. You know how important the lay of the land is in any battle. Let's find that guide and get him to take us up in the mountains. From there we can get a bird's eye view of the future battle scene.

ALEXANDER:

That's a GREAT idea! We might find out something useful. In any case, we'll have fun mountain climbing. It'll do me good to get away from all this fuss. The two of us together, having fun. Just like it used to be!

(They put their arms around each other's shoulders and walk off, laughing together like boys going on an adventure.)

_____

SCENE FIVE----- "LOVING YOU IS BETTER THAN ANY MAN I'VE HAD!"

MARCH 22, 333 B.C.

CHARACTERS:

NARRATOR
FIRST MOUNTAIN WOMAN
SECOND MOUNTAIN WOMAN
CHASE
ALEXANDER
HEPHAISTON
LITTLE GIRL
ONE EYE
SECOND VILLAGE MAN
THIRD VILLAGE MAN

Teacher, please say, "I need the following characters up here in the stage area: FIRST MOUNTAIN WOMAN and SECOND MOUNTAIN WOMAN. CHASE is off stage, ready to enter. On the other side, off stage are: LITTLE GIRL, ONE EYE, SECOND VILLAGE MAN, THIRD VILLAGE MAN. ALEXANDER AND HEPHAISTON are off stage, ready to come in at the end. The NARRATOR stands apart, alone."

NARRATOR:
First and Second Mountain Woman are inside their home, a two-roomed building made of field stone and roofed with straw. They are sitting on a pile of furs near a fireplace. Both of them are weaving, using a hand loom. They continue to weave as they talk.

FIRST MOUNTAIN WOMAN:
Loving you is better than any man I've had.

SECOND MOUNTAIN WOMAN:
We fit together, don't we, like an old glove on your hand.

FIRST MOUNTAIN WOMAN:
You meet my needs more than my husband did. When he was killed, I thought I'd never be happy again, but I'm much happier with you now.   When we make love, you make me glow all over. You go slow and easy, and you tell me that you love me. He was too fast and hard, and never said a word. He was DONE before I got started!
(She laughs a little at this and Second Mountain Woman then laughs too.)

SECOND MOUNTAIN WOMAN:
Yes, men are always in a hurry, aren't they? Only women know what women need.

FIRST MOUNTAIN WOMAN:
And you don't care how old I am. My husband was always looking around for a younger woman. I got so sick of that. He always said, "Your baby days are almost over ". That was all he cared about in me.

SECOND MOUNTAIN WOMAN:

I love your gray hair and your wise eyes. They show you're old enough to know how to take care of me!

FIRST MOUNTAIN WOMAN:

(Again they laugh together, then kiss each other gently for a moment.)
These eyes have seen a lot, that's for sure. I've learned some things. I know the herbs that ease your pain.

SECOND MOUNTAIN WOMAN:

You're wise in many other ways too. Look at our home! We're warm because you know how to build a good fire place. Look at these soft furs we're sitting on. We have them because you're a great hunter.

FIRST MOUNTAIN WOMAN:

Well, you do all the cooking, Sweetheart. We eat well because you try out new things all the time. Who else would have thought to put wild honey in most of what we eat?

SECOND MOUNTAIN WOMAN:

While we're talking all nice like this, what about our boy, Chase? Hasn't he turned out well? People said two mothers and no dad would produce a weak boy, but look at ours. He's the best one in the village and everybody knows it!

FIRST MOUNTAIN WOMAN:

He is, isn't he, even if they don't like to SAY it. The men around here still don't like us much. They resent how well he hunts. He's earned his nickname, hasn't he? He can chase down any animal. I'll bet no other family in the village eats as well as we do. I think I hear him now.

(A noise is heard outside and Chase comes in with a big, long haired dog that looks like a wolf. He is carrying a dead wild sheep over his shoulder.)

CHASE:

(He speaks with a strong, cheerful tone in his voice, and he's very handsome.)

Hello,Mothers! I've brought home supper! I'm as hungry as a new born lamb. (*The dog barks.*) I guess that means Wolf is hungry too. He deserves all he wants because he found this sheep for me.

We were off some place in the high country where we almost never go. Wolf ran off after a rabbit. I followed him into this big, long open place between two mountains. Normally this area is full of ice and snow all year round, but it's been so WARM this winter that there's almost no ice there. Now you can see that there's this long, skinny valley between the mountains. It was probably formed by the stream that runs down the middle of it, I guess.

Anyway, I followed Wolf down the valley ; the valley goes on for as far as I could see, all the way to the flat plains, to the big river. The valley was full of game, and they'd never even seen a human so they were just standing around looking at me! I didn't have to chase at all! It was getting late, so I got this one and here it is---for us to eat!

(*A fast knock is heard, then in rushes a little girl, out of breath. The women put down their weaving to go to the girl whom they hug.*)

LITTLE GIRL:

My mom told me to run here fast, and I sure did. Mother said your husband's back, and he and some others are headed this way right now. She said the men have weapons. I'm sorry but I can't stay to help you fight the bad men; Mother told me I have to get home as fast as I can.

(*She leaves but looks back over her shoulder because she's worried about her friends.*)

SECOND MOUNTAIN WOMAN:

(*Suddenly her face is filled with fear.*)

That son of a bitch is here to KILL me. Last time I saw him, he said he'd kill me, if I ever left him again. That was many moons ago, but I can still see his one eye filled with hate. I've got to get out of here!

FIRST MOUNTAIN WOMAN

(*She puts her arm protectively around Second Woman.*)

No you don't. This is your home now. I'll MURDER the son of a bitch

if he tries to hurt you. He's never going to lay a hand on you again! Hide over there behind those things. It's better if he doesn't see you at all. Now where's my spear? Oh, there it is.
(First Mountain Woman picks up a wooden spear, while Second Mountain Woman hides in a corner.)

CHASE:
(He puts his strong arm around First Mountain Woman.)

I'll help you take care of One Eye and his friends.   You know I'm as big as they are now, and a lot faster. I'll knock the bastards down, and kill them if I have to. Hand me my spear, will you? I left it by the door. I've got my sharp stone knife right here. *(He gets it out.)*

(One Eye,Second and Third Village Men push open the door. One Eye has big wooden club, plus a stone knife. The other two have short wooden spears. All look mean and hateful.)

ONE EYE:
Where's my goddam wife? I know she's here. I want my woman NOW!

FIRST MOUNTAIN WOMAN:
(She's yelling and holding up her spear at him.)

 She's NOT your woman anymore.   Get out of here, you asshole!

ONE EYE:
(He's screaming with rage and gets his club ready to swing.)

The Hell she's not! She BELONGS to me, like this club does. No old woman-lover is going to take my wife from me.

FIRST MOUNTAIN WOMAN:

She doesn't belong to anybody but herself.   And she wants to be here with me.

CHASE:
(He holds his knife out,ready to fight.)
And ME! We three are a family, and we're going to stay a family. Get out of here right now.

ONE EYE:
(He makes a fist with his free hand.)
You're not a REAL family, you stupid shit; you're just two woman-lovers and a kid. A family is a man, a woman, and their kids--- that's the way it's got to be. There's no other way.

SECOND VILLAGE MAN:
You tell 'em, One Eye! A woman's NOTHING without a man.

THIRD VILLAGE MAN:
Don't you fools know shit? How do you think a baby's made? You have to have a man and woman!

FIRST MOUNTAIN WOMAN:
Let's take this fight out of door. We're going to need a lot of room to settle this.

ONE EYE:
(He shrugs his shoulders in the "I don't care" gesture.)

I don't care where we fight, but we're gonna beat your ass!
Hey, why don't you bring out my woman, so she can watch me win her back? I know she's hiding some where close.

SECOND MOUNTAIN WOMAN:
(She comes out and goes to her family so they stand together. Then she addresses everyone.)

I'm here, One Eye, and I'm NOT your woman! Yes, let's go outside to fight.
.

(They all go outside. Suddenly up rides Alexander the Great and his partner, Hephaiston. Both are wearing helmets and breast plates; both have their short swords out, ready for action.   They see there's trouble so they come over to the mountain people.)

ALEXANDER:
What's going on here, People? It looks to me like you men with clubs are trying to bully these women. I don't allow that sort of thing.

ONE EYE:
Who are you to tell us what to do? We're a free mountain tribe. We're not ruled by you Persians.

HEPHAISTON:
We're not Persians; we're GREEKS. This is our leader ALEXANDER, KING OF MACEDON. He's the most famous fighter in world. You do what he says, or we'll kill you on the spot.

SECOND MOUNTAIN MAN:
(He puts his arm up to sort of protect his face,as from a god.   His face is full of terror. He knells down to Alexander.)

Don't kill me, Sir. Please don't kill me.   Even up here in the mountains, we've heard people talk about you. You have a big army, and you NEVER loose a fight.

THIRD MOUNTAIN MAN:
(His face shows fear too, as he kneels down.)

People say you're a GOD, Sir. Please don't send lightning to destroy us. If you want to kill someone, kill One Eye here. This hurting women stuff was all his idea; he's the one to blame.

ONE EYE:

Thanks for NOTHING, guys. I don't have much choice I guess. I'm plenty tough but I can't fight a god. I'll kneel to you too.

HEPHAISTON:
(He smiles a little at how easily the bullies caved in.)

Now that's more like it. You men just saved your lives.

ALEXANDER:
(He speaks in a loud, firm voice, and frowns.)

I ORDER you cowards to leave these people alone in the future. Treat them with respect. I'm a god you know. *(He winks secretly at Hephaiston.)* I'll know if you disobey me. You don't want to see my fury! Now get out of here.
(They exit.)
(Now he speaks in a kind, friendly voice to the mountain women and the boy.)

Your trouble is over, my friends. Those cowards are afraid of me. You're safe.

And you can pay me back right now. My friend and I are looking for a way to get some of my soldiers through these mountains. I've heard there's supposed to be a path, but it's always blocked by ice.

CHASE:
(His face lights up with joy that he can help these heroes.)

Great King, I'm called Chase because I've chased down game in these mountains ALL MY LIFE!

ALEXANDER:
(He smiles good naturally.)

As long as that? What do you know about a pass and what about the ice?

CHASE:

Great King, I have good news for you. Yes, there's a path; and I can lead you to it! Even better, the ice is GONE right now. It's been so warm this winter that there's no ice at all. I was just there. Grass is starting to come up on the path.

ALEXANDER:
(He gets off from his horse and goes up to the boy and puts his hands on the boy's shoulders, looking into his face. Hephaiston dismounts too.)

That's great, Chase! Now tell me about the path. How far does it go and how wide is it?

CHASE:
Great King, I followed it three years ago when there wasn't any ice for a short while. I followed it all the way! It leads completely through the mountains and ends up on the plain, where the big river is.

ALEXANDER:
So far so good. Now how wide is the path?

CHASE:
It varies of course, but it's pretty wide. I'd say at its most narrow place, it's wide enough for three or four horses to ride abreast.

ALEXANDER:
(He gives Chase a bear hug and a kiss on both cheeks.)

May the gods bless you, Chase, for this great news!
Hesphaiston, please give Chase two of the gold coins we just had made, the ones with my face on them. He can spend one coin, and keep the other. He can tell his grandchildren, "ALEXANDER gave this to me."

HEPHAISTON:
I'm happy about this news of course, but how are you going to use Chase's pass? We can't march men up here fast enough for the coming battle, can we?

ALEXANDER:

Perhaps not. But what if there's another choice, a faster alternative to our MEN?

SCENE SIX------------" THE TRANSGENDERED ONE "

MARCH 19, 333 B.C.--- EARLY IN THE MORNING

CHARACTERS:

KING DARIUS OF THE PERSIAN EMPIRE
TRANSGENDERED PRIEST
NARRATOR

Teacher, please say, " Up here in our stage area, I need King Darius and Transgendered Priest and Narrator."

NARRATOR:

It's March 19, 333 B.C. early in the morning, a few days before the big battle. We're now in the vast camp of the Persian King of Kings. Hundreds of luxurious tents in bright blue and purple are near its center. In one of these are King Darius and Transgendered Priest. The King of Kings is about 40 years old. He's handsome in a stern way, with long black hair and beard, both tightly curled. He wears trousers, with a short robe over them. The pants are emerald green velvet, while the robe is royal purple embroidered with many large emerald and pearls. He has on the Mithra , the crown of the Persian Empire.

The other person with him is also about 40. This person has long, flowing hair surrounding a pretty face with lots of make-up on. The person looks entirely like a woman, except for rather broad shoulders. She's wearing a dress decorated with male and female symbols intertwined.

KING DARIUS:

(He raises his hands in the air, in prayer. In front of him is incense burning to make a rich,musky smell.)

Holy TRANSGENDERED One, male and female, hear my royal prayer. I am Darius, KING of Kings. I rule the Persian Empire in your name.

I need your help, great TWO IN ONE TOGETHER. The Greek barbarians are causing me serious trouble. Their Alexander has broken into Asia , like a thief at midnight. He's stolen part of my Empire, and I MUST get it back. Soon there will be a big battle. Please help my army crush him, like the little cockroach he is.

If you do this for me, I promise I'll change the Empire's religion; we'll worship only YOU. Our old god has deserted us. If you help me, I'll build many temples for you. Each will have a statue of you as the Pregnant Women, in white stone, with your hundred breasts all over. On the other side will be you as Male Member, a thick, long column of black stone. The whole Empire will see your COMPLETENESS, Great Cybele, FATHER/MOTHER of us all!

TRANSGENDERED PRIEST:

Great King of Kings, she/he will hear you, I am sure. She likes the fact that for religious support, you are worshiping here in her tent, instead of in the fire temple you used to bring on your wars. She's happy that you like her better than your old Zorastorian religion with its fire worship.

KING DARIUS:

Priest, I want to get her support as much as I can. What would the Transgendered One like me to do?

TRANSGENDERED PRIEST:

She/He would like it most if you would come to one of our FIXING UP ceremonies.

KING DARIUS:

What in the world is that, Priest?

TRANSGENDERED PRIEST:

You remember, don't you? I told you this before, but I think you were smoking opium at the time. The Fixing Up is when we help people who want to CHANGE their gender. You remember when I told you there are some people in the world who feel trapped in the wrong body? They may have a male member, but inside they feel like a girl. Or they might be born with female breasts, but they know in their hearts that they're really a man.

In this ceremony, we FIX THEM UP. We make them into the gender that they choose.

DARIUS:

Yes, I remember that now. I think it did slip my mind because I was doing opium. Are you sure doing this is a good thing? And exactly HOW do you do it?

TRANSGENDERED PRIEST:

I know it does sound odd, but it can help some people a lot. ME for example! I was born with a penis and seemed like the other baby boys at first, but soon it became clear that I was different. When I was given a choice of toys, I choose the doll and not the little sword. I always played with the girls, unless my dad caught me. He'd yell at me and beat me, but I'd go back to the girls as soon as he left. I couldn't help it; it just seemed I was born this way, a girl trapped in the body of a boy.

DARIUS:

Yes, go on. It must have been bad for you.

TRANSGENDERED PRIEST:

It was, worse than you can know. I tried to kill myself when I was ten.

DARIUS:

Then what happened?

TRANSGENDERED PRIEST:

I was on my own now because my father had already thrown me out of his house. Well, I was in the great city of Damascus, walking down the street called "Straight". That was an ironic name for me, wasn't it? *(He laughs a little)*

So, anyway, I was walking down "Straight Street", when I saw the big statue of Cybele, the Mother/Father of us all. A priest there told me this religion believed that gender was much more complex than my dad back home said.

The Cybele priest said male and female was more like a line with totally male at one end, with totally female at the other end, and with many different blends in between.   He said most people could find out fairly easily where they belonged on the line, if only they did not worry about labels, instead just dressed and did what felt right for them.

Are you getting bored, Great King?

KING DARIUS:

Certainly not! This is very interesting to me. I rather liked dolls myself when I was a little boy.

TRANSGENDERED PRIEST:

(He laughs a little in a sympathetic way.)

Yes, I think we're all more complex inside than we usually like to admit. Gender isn't EITHER/OR , not nearly as much as most people think. Should I go on with my story?

KING DARIUS:

Please do.

TRANSGENDERED PRIEST:

Well, when I told the Cybele priest about my life, he said his religion could help me. First we talked about it for several weeks, and when he saw how much I was a girl except for my penis, he said that Cybele could solve the problem. He said that in some extreme cases like mine, the best thing to do was to have an operation.

KING DARIUS:
(He looks worried.)

To do what exactly?

TRANSGENDERED PRIEST:
To remove my male parts. To CUT THEM OFF!

KING DARIUS:
(His face shows how deeply he's shocked.)
How AWEFUL!

TRANSGENDERED PRIEST:
It was of course; at first it hurt so much, but they had medicine to help me heal pretty fast. From then on, I wore girls' clothing, and took a girl's name. I learned to weave and sew. I loved it. It all felt so easy, so right for me.

Later on, I became a priest myself so I could help others who were confused about gender issues. Lots of young people come to me and some older ones do too.

Almost all of them find out who they feel comfortable being WITHOUT an operation of course. The operation is a very serious thing that only should be used if the situation really needs such an extreme solution. I keep stressing that to them.

I've found that most young people just need to let themselves do what comes natural to them. Some boys decide they like to wear a little make-up, or maybe a lot of it sometimes. Some like to dress entirely like girls. They let themselves be graceful with their bodies. You know---limp wrists, one arm at one side, that sort of thing.

They often enjoy the company of other boys like themselves. A lot of time they become so much happier because now they don't have to pretend to be as manly as an athlete or soldier.   They often feel free for the first time, and they feel happy, silly even---they laugh a lot.   I guess this is why they're called GAY, don't you think?

KING DARIUS:

That could be it I suppose. By the way, the ones like you, the men who

don't have balls and dress like women---- who do you people LIKE?
And who do you want to marry?

TRANSGENDERED PRIEST:

Personally, I like older men, guys with nice big bellies and with hair
like bears, but most of them don't like me. I'd take any decent man
who'd be nice to me, and love me for who I am.

KING DARIUS:

I hope you find one, I really do. I guess I was more fortunate than
you. When I was ten, I tried sex with girls and with boys. I found out
it all felt good to me.
    And of course people let me do anything I wanted with both
sexes, as long as I didn't hurt someone. I was going to be the KING
after all! I had a LOT of fun!

TRANSGENDERED PRIEST:

Yes, Your Majesty, you were very fortunate to know you were bi-
sexual early in your life, and you were even more fortunate to be able
to experiment sexually all you wanted. Most of all, you were lucky to
HAVE NO ONE MAKE YOU ASHAMED OF WHO YOU ARE. I wish we
all were blessed like that. I think it would be good if every young
person could find out what he/she liked by having sex all they want.
Adolescence would be a lot easier---and a WHOLE lot more fun!

DARIUS:
(*He sort of chuckles and smiles.*)

I COULD decree free love for the young! They'd love me for it, but of
course all those fussy old fire-worshipping Magi---they'd HATE young
people having fun. They'd get rid of me for sure! So that idea won't
work right now I'm afraid.

TRANSGENDERED PRIEST:
I guess not, Great King, but you can at least be tolerant of a wide

variety of sexual practices, don't you think? You could order everyone to let everyone else be who they are, and you could order people to RESPECT each other: no bullying and no hate crimes, and no talking mean.

DARIUS:
I could, couldn't I? Sexual tolerance and mutual respect---they could become the law.

And come to think of it, I already am tolerant, am I not? Look at what I allow my twin sister to do. She's not BI like me---she's a total lesbian, even if she does look and act like a normal woman. She's very FEMININE, lipstick and all, but she only likes her own gender when it comes to sex.

TRANSGENDERED PRIEST:

Yes, I've seen her. She's very, very beautiful. After all, she's your twin sister, Sir!   She's as good looking for a woman, as you are for a man.

DARIUS:

Thank you,Priest. Speaking of my sister, I have another job for you. You remember how I had you spy on the Queen Mother, the great Sisygambis, several months ago. You were perfect to spy on her because you're allowed to be where the women are; you can't have sex with them, and of course you dress like women so you blend right in.   I needed you to listen while she talked to her friends to see if she really does support me. I've always been afraid she doesn't think much of me, if the truth were known.

TRANSGENDERED PRIEST:
(He sounds sad,remembering this.)

Yes, of course I remember, Sir. It was terrible to have to tell you that she said good things about General Memnon, but only BAD   things about you.

DARIUS:
(He puts his head down a bit and looks sad for a moment or two.)

It still hurts me---that my own mother doesn't like me much. I've heard her say she wished that my sister had been the boy, so she could have inherited job of being the King of Kings.

But back to the immediate business. I want you to spy on my sister now. My mother would never actually DO anything to get me off the throne, but I'm afraid my SISTER is planning that right now.   One of my concubines last night told me, while we were in bed, that she overheard my sister say she plans on meeting General Memnon this afternoon to figure out how to get rid of me.

 I want you, Priest, to learn what you can, and then send me word by a secret messenger. Go at once. My royal life may depend on you.

TRANSGENDERED PRIEST:
As you say, I do, Your Majesty. Do you know where she is right now?

DARIUS:
She's over in the Woman's Part of course, in her portable garden probably, talking with her smart friends.
     Now where's my opium pipe? All this serious business has worn me out. I need a nice, deep smoke!
     Say, by the way, don't wear that fancy dress you have on now. Change to something simpler so you look more like a servant. And keep you voice up high, like you're doing now.

TRANSGENDERED PRIEST:
(He says this in a sort of "queeny" way: with amused sarcasm.)

Begging Your Majesty's pardon, but I think I KNOW how to be a woman. I've had some practice, you know.

SCENE SEVEN-------- " A WOMAN WILL RULE THE WORLD? "

MARCH 19, 333 B.C.--- LATE IN THE AFTERNOON

CHARACTERS:

TRANSGENDERED PRIEST
MAID
ROYAL TWIN
GENERAL MEMNON
PRINCESS ANN
QUEEN MOTHER SISYGAMBIS
FIRST ROYAL GIRL
SECOND ROYAL GIRL
THIRD ROYAL GIRL
FOURTH ROYAL GIRL
KING DARIUS
FIRST SOLDIER
SECOND SOLDIER
FIRST GENERAL
SECOND GENERAL
NARRATOR

Teacher please say, " Up here in front, I need: the Narrator, standing alone, and Transgendered Priest and Maid ,standing, as servants, with Royal Twin and General Memnon sitting at a silver table. Princess Ann is offstage, ready to come in soon.

Queen Mother Sisygambis and the Royal Girls are offstage, ready to enter. King Darius with two soldiers are also waiting to enter at the end of the scene. First General and Second General are also offstage,waiting to come in at the very last."

_____

TRANSGENDERED PRIEST:
Honey, why don't you let me carry that heavy tray for you? You look a bit tired.

MAID:
Who are you anyway? What happened to old Sarah?

TRANSGENDERED PRIEST:
I'm her substitute today. They told me she's come down with a fever.

MAID:
She WAS feeling bad yesterday. Well, I'm glad you're here. Just take this fruit tray to the Royal Twin. I'll go get the rest.

(He comes up silently to the royal table, bows low, but no one notices. He puts down the fruit, then moves away but not too far, into a shaded corner where he appears to be working with potted plants, to give himself a cover as he spies.)

NARRATOR:
Seated at a solid silver table are the ROYAL TWIN and GENERAL MEMNON, who is wearing a wig of long hair with a large silk shawl over most of his face. With his strong manly face, he looks ridiculous! He wears a blue embroidered dress, with a great deal of silver jewelry, including big dangling ear rings.

ROYAL TWIN:
(She laughs quietly at him.)

General Memnon, you look quite lovely today. I especially like your ear rings!

GENERAL MEMNON:

Thank you, Your Royal Highness, but please let's do our business before someone recognizes me. I'm a dead man if one of your ladies figures out I'm a man; a man caught in the Women's Part is always killed of course.

ROYAL TWIN:

Believe me, Memnon, no one would recognize you in that wig. You

look quite convincing! But of course you're right about business.
(She starts to whisper now.)
Have you decided what's the best way to KILL my brother?

GENERAL MEMNON:

Yes, M'am, I have. I've forced one of his bodyguards to promise to stab him with a lance as soon as the battle's fighting gets near the king. I've kidnapped the man's whole family and told him they're dead unless the King is. He'll do it I'm sure. Of course the other bodyguards will kill him, but that's HIS problem.

Then I'll put myself in charge. If the King stays in charge, we'll lose. With my leadership and yours, we'll WIN. You always should have ruled, and now you will.   A woman will rule the world!

ROYAL TWIN:
(She stands up to embrace him and shake his hand. She's on fire with energy and ambition.)

I will indeed. A WOMAN will rule the world!
(Calming down, she returns to practical things.)

General, there's one more thing. I'd like to get my mother's approval for what we plan on doing, or at least her passive acceptance. It won't be as hard as you'd think, because she knows how many mistakes my brother has made recently. She's afraid we may loose this war because of him.

So I'd like you to go away for a little while, and then come back here in about an hour when Mother's supposed to pay me a visit. Then you can help convince her that to save our country we have to dispose of my brother.

GENERAL MEMNON:
Yes, your Royal Highness. I'll walk around your beautiful flower garden over there.   I raise tulips like those at home. I'd like to see how yours are doing in all those big pots. It won't take too long. I'll be back in time to meet with your royal mother. I'll see you soon.
(He leaves.)

TRANSGENDERED PRIEST:
(He is talking to himself.)

I have to get this to King Darius at once, so he can catch Memnon while he's still here in the Women's Part. Finding Memnon here will give the King a easy excuse to kill him on the spot.
    Now where is that cute little messenger?

NARRATOR:

The Royal Twin continues with her meal. She picks up a scroll and starts to read it. In comes a beautiful woman who looks about 40. From her elegant but simple clothes, you can tell she's a princess. She's carrying a small sculpture that looks like several geometric shapes floating together. She puts the statue on a nearby small table. She comes up behind Royal Twin who is deep in her reading. She smells her hair slightly, then kisses it tenderly.

PRINCESS ANN:
I miss the way your hair smells.

ROYAL TWIN:
(She gets up and hugs Ann warmly, then pulls back a little to look at her face.)

I miss your blue, blue eyes. Let me look at you! It's been too long. How long has it been--- six months?

PRINCESS ANN:
More like a year.
(She looks around, getting a frown on her face.)
What have you been up to? Why are you with all these men?

ROYAL TWIN:

It's not so bad here in the Women's Part; no men are allowed here and I've made it look like home. Look at all the flowering shrubs and ferns I have in pots. It's my portable garden. I even have some of my birds---see that peacock over there? Remember when it bit your hand?

But to answer your question, we're at war of course. Alexander of Macedon has taken over half of our empire. We're trying to stop him here. There'll be a big battle in a few days.

Now please don't get upset. I remember how you hate violence. I'll get you out of here before the fighting starts.

But tell me about yourself. You're looking wonderful, RADIANT almost. You haven't aged a bit. You still have that tom-boy charm you had when we were first together. What do you have there? What's that thing you put on the table?

PRINCESS ANN:
(She smiles, full of enthusiasm.)
It's for you. I found it in a shop back home. They told me it was carved by a WOMAN, and her name was Pelton. That was all they knew about it.

Don't you just LOVE it? It's so feminine somehow. It's smooth and full of understated curves, like YOU when we first met.
(She goes on, lost in her own enthusiasm.)
Last night I wrote a poem for you. As I felt the statue, these words came into my mind.

Ideas, countless as the stars,
Live and die in us.
Flowing in fields, fast and slow,
Swirling as they go.
Glowing purples, pinks
Blending together,
Sowing,
Growing.

Then looming gloom,
Silently moves in,
Like a storm cloud in the sky.
But small, bright stars
Shine through too.

Then they fade away....
To be born again another day?

(Ann looks expectantly at Royal Twin who starts to frown and shake her head "no" slightly.)

Well, tell me what you think. I can see from your face that something's bothering you.

ROYAL TWIN:
I like some things about your poem; it's structure is strong, and your sound repetition works for me....

PRINCESS ANN:
(Ann is frowning a little now, worried.)

BUT? But what? What don't you like? Tell me what you're thinking.

ROYAL TWIN:
Well, you asked for it. First of all, it's too vague, too abstract, too "flowing, glowing" as you put it. I think our Persian poetry should be concrete. It should be about actual people, ROYAL people to be precise. The ancient poems are always about our fighting kings and all the brave things they do and say. That's the way yours should be.

   Secondly, if you want me to be honest, I don't like the STATUE.   I don't like it at all. What exactly IS it? What's it supposed to be? Our Persian art should portray REAL things, you know, kings fighting lions, things like that---not just smooth, curving shapes. Our empire's art has always been ROYAL. That's the way it's supposed to be. That's who we are; that's who we have always been.

PRINCESS ANN:
(Of course she's getting angry, but she tries to sound calm and open-minded.)

You're welcome to your opinion of course, but I have to disagree. You're right about our old art, but why can't artists try something NEW? *(She points to the statue.)* Like that smooth, simple thing?

ROYAL TWIN:
(Her face expressions and her voice tone show she's getting angry, but trying to control it.)

They can't "try something new" because old is just BETTER. Our ancient traditions are what make us GREAT.   Our art is supposed to express what our group has always believed in. I don't like this new INDIVIDUALISM at all. It's the whole GROUP that counts---not the separate little people. INDIVIDUALISM, newness--- that's the awful GREEK IDEA.   Each individual a KING?   That's nonsense! What would happen to our upper class if this idea, like a plague, spread across the Empire?

PRINCESS ANN:
(Now she's really mad and her face and voice show it.)

So it's only tradition that matters? The GROUP is what matters? The individual not at all?
　　　Where does that leave us lesbians, I'd like to know? Persian tradition says women should worship men and do nothing but have their babies. What about you and me? Don't we want INDIVIDUAL choice? Don't we NEED to fight the tyranny of the group?
　　　(She's almost screaming now.) We're a MINORITY after all! Have you LOST YOUR MIND?

ROYAL TWIN:
How DARE you raise your voice to me! Now I remember why we broke up.   You don't KNOW YOUR PLACE!

PRINCESS ANN:
Yes, I remember the break up too. You never respected what I had to say. You never really LISTENED to me at all. I didn't matter as much as you.   You always had to be on TOP!
(She picks up the statue and walks away without looking back.)
Well, you're NOT on top of me any more.   I'm leaving. Goodbye forever!

ROYAL TWIN:

(She looks with anger at Ann as she leaves, then puts on her calm, official face to get back to business. At first she is talking softly to herself.)

I don't have time to deal with her emotions, not right now. I've got an empire to run.

NARRATOR:
She hears the rustle of a large curtain behind her then stands up and turns to meet her mother and her four young nieces as they enter. Queen Mother Sisygambis is 80 years old, but still beautiful in her dignity, like Queen Elizabeth the Second. She wears a many layered outfit made of silver cloth with diamonds sewed all over it. She has a matching veil that is pulled back now because she's in the Women's Part. Royal Sister kisses each of her guests with a kiss on both cheeks. She and her mother also share a rather stiff hug. The nieces stand back a way, shy and not very interested in what the adults are doing. They whisper to each other and giggle a little.

ROYAL TWIN:
Mother, on time as usual. You've always been careful with your time; no wonder I am too.

SISYGAMBIS:
(She speaks in a cold, authoritative voice, and holds herself with a stiff dignity, head held high and shoulders back.)

Of course you are. You HAVE to be, to rule an empire. I trained you and your twin almost from birth to work hard and work well. Unfortunately, he didn't learn it like you did.

ROYAL TWIN:

Mother, we have some very important business about him to finish right now. It's quite complicated I fear. It'll be boring for the girls.
      Girls, why don't you all pick up the peacock food I have in the golden basket over there and go out into the garden to feed the birds?

FIRST ROYAL GIRL:

Yes, Auntie, but we're AFRAID of your birds. Last time we were here, your parrot swore at us, then the mean thing bit my hand.

SECOND ROYAL GIRL:
(She starts to giggle at the memory.)

You certainly looked like a silly goose that day! You were on the floor crying hard, and the bird kept right on cussing you. You were so mad!

THIRD ROYAL GIRL:
You giggle too much. I get so sick of it!

FOURTH ROYAL GIRL:
(She pinches Third Royal Girl on the cheek, but does it so the adults don't notice.)
Shut up, stupid!

SISYGAMBIS:

That's a good idea, Daughter.
  Girls, pull your shawl up over your heads and go outside. It's still rather cold today.

(The four girls bow silently, pull up their shawls, pick up the gold basket, and leave giggling.)

ROYAL TWIN:

 Mother, have your spies told you what we've been planning?

SISYGAMBIS:
Perhaps.

ROYAL TWIN:
Will you support us, or at least keep quiet?

SISYGAMBIS:
I have nothing to say to that.

ROYAL TWIN:
Mother, I have some idea how hard this must be for you.

SISYGAMBIS:
No, you don't. Women like you have no children.

ROYAL TWIN:
Maybe I don't have children, but I do know that I love our country with all my heart. And our country is very close to DISASTER. If my brother continues to make big mistakes like he's been doing, Alexander will conquer us soon. If General Memnon and I take over, we can save our country before it's too late. I have the brains and the energy to BEAT that Greek upstart!

SISYGAMBIS:

(She slowly nods yes but still looks stern, like she hates to say what she says. She says it slowly.)

You DO I know. You should have been the KING of Kings. If our Persian laws weren't made by men, YOU would have been King. After all, you came out of my womb before he did. YOU should have inherited the throne.

ROYAL TWIN:
Thank you, Mother. I know that was very hard for you to say. I KNOW you see that I have no choice in this. It's either your son or your country: one of them MUST die soon.

SISYGAMBIS:
(Silent tears begin to fall from her eyes. She looks deeply sad.)

No mother should have to make this choice. He's my SON, after all, my baby boy. How can I be involved in his murder?
(She starts to cry.)

ROYAL TWIN:

Mother, you always taught us that the PERSIAN WAY is to value your country more than ANYTHING; more than your friends, and more than your family too, and more than yourself of course.

      The COUNTRY must survive. We're like wild horses in this way; sometimes the individual must die so that the herd lives on. The GROUP counts the most. You taught us that, Mother, with your Mother's milk.

SISYGAMBIS:

I know I did. I taught you that, like my mother taught me, and hers taught her before.
(She looks down and is silent for a long time, then she looks up at her daughter and says with some peace in her voice now.)

Yes, I have to support you. PERSIA must live on.

(General Memnon is hiding off to one side, silently listening, like a spy. The royals are unaware of him.)

ROYAL TWIN:

Mother, you decided that like the true Persian Queen you are. Now would you please go find his daughters in the garden and take them away from here? I don't want them to know anything about all this mess.

SISYGAMBIS:

Yes, that's best. I certainly could use some fresh air after all this. Goodbye, Daughter. I just can't bring myself to kiss you right now.
(She leaves without kissing her daughter.)
(General Memnon now comes out of hiding. He comes up to Royal Twin, and bows to her very low, from the waist. He is smiling.)

GENERAL MEMNON:

My, that went better than I expected. I was afraid we might have more trouble with your mother. I'm pleased she's going along with us. Let's celebrate with a drink!

NARRATOR:

General Memnon goes to the table and starts to pour from a wine bottle into a golden cup, shaped like a horn on its side. From the other side, King Darius and First Soldier and Second Soldier rush in, swords in their hands. King Darius goes up to General Memnon, who has no weapon since he's dressed as a woman.

KING DARIUS:

You goddamned TRAITOR! Arrest him at once, men, and put a gag on his mouth. And take that stupid wig off of him. I don't want to hear his lying voice ever again. Damn him to Hell, he was my best general, and I thought he was my friend.

Tell everyone that I found him here in the Woman's Part, dressed like a goddamned woman. Everyone knows that's an instant death. I don't want people to know that my top general was a traitor. It would hurt morale.

Take him to the prison area. Tell the men in charge that he gets THE DEATH OF A THOUSAND CUTS. Tell them I'll be there to help cut him up, just as soon as I'm done here.

FIRST SOLDIER:

Yes, Your Majesty.

SECOND SOLDIER:

We hear and we obey, Great King.

ROYAL TWIN:

What about me, Brother? Are you going to kill me too?

KING DARIUS:

No, I certainly feel like it right now, but I CAN'T. It would be against Persian tradition: a royal woman should NEVER be put to death. Never, not even when they commit treason, as you have done.

I think I'll just put you away some place where you can't cause me any more trouble. The palace at Susa might be the right place; it's isolated---way up in the mountains, far from anyone that matters.

GUARDS! Come here at once! Take her to the prison area for now.

(Two very tall black women, Tutsi people from Africa, come up and bow silently to the King. They tie Royal Twin's hands behind her back, then gag her mouth and lead her off to jail.)

(In come First General and Second General, both with maps in their hands, which they put on a table.)

FIRST GENERAL:
We're here as you ordered, Your Majesty, and we have brought our maps as you can see.

SECOND GENERAL:
Where is General Memnon, Sir? We can't have a full staff meeting without the Head General. He always has the best ideas,doesn't he?

KING DARIUS:
(He talks in an everyday tone of voice, like it's no big deal.)

He DID perhaps, but will no more. I just now caught him here in the Women's Part without my permission, so I've ordered the DEATH OF A THOUSAND CUTS for him. They're doing it as we speak.

FIRST GENERAL:
You know best, Your Majesty. Will YOU lead this staff conference then, Sir?

KING DARIUS:
Of course I will. I always should have. I left too much to that man. Now what do I do first?

SECOND GENERAL:
Your Majesty, we have to make the final plans for the coming battle. Do you want us to take an offensive blow first?

KING DARIUS:
Yes, let's attack them. It'll make me look more manly. First we'll send in our foot soldiers. We have probably ten times as many as they have. I admit they have breastplates and helmets, and we have only

CLOTH coats and hats, but we can take huge loses, then send in another 20,000 men, then do it again when those are gone.

After the foot soldiers soften them up, you two generals can lead the cavalry charge. Our brave knights can gallup up to the Greeks and smash through their front line. If many of our men on horseback get killed, we'll send in more, then more. After all we have way more cavalry than they do.

FIRST GENERAL:
What if Alexander comes out to fight our cavalry? His horsemen are very brave or so say our spies.

KING DARIUS:

It won't matter how brave they are. Our horsemen out number theirs five to one at least. The Greeks will DROWN in our Persian sea of horses.

SECOND GENERAL:
Your Majesty, what are you going to do with those camels you had brought in from Arabia?

KING DARIUS:
Well, they can join our horsemen, can't they? First we'll use the horsemen, then we'll send in all the camels too. Those strange looking creatures will scare the hell out of the dumb Greeks!

FIRST GENERAL:
What about those big, fat animals you brought all the way from India? I think they're called elephants.

KING DARIUS:
We can save them for the END! When the Greeks are getting tired, we'll attack them with our elephants. That will scare the Greeks so badly, Alexander will try to find me, so he can surrender. He'll find out that I deserve to be the king of kings. He'll be sorry he ever picked a fight with ME!

SCENE SEVEN---------"THE LESBIAN LEGION"

TIME--- MARCH 20, 333 B.C.

CHARACTERS:

NARRATOR
VILLAGE MOTHER
FIRST VILLAGE WOMAN
SECOND VILLAGE WOMAN
VILLAGE HUSBAND
LIONGUARD
QUEEN SAPPHO THE TENTH
LYDIA
NURSE
LYDIA'S FRIEND
OTHER NURSE
FIRST GIRL
FIRST WOMAN (in Lesbian Legion)
SECOND WOMAN (in Lesbian Legion)

> TEACHER PLEASE SAY, " Right now, I want only the following characters to come up here to the stage area: NARRATOR, VILLAGE MOTHER , FIRST VILLAGE WOMAN, SECOND VILLAGE WOMAN, and HUSBAND. They stand close together. LIONGUARD is by herself, a little way off. NARRATOR stands alone at one side."

NARRATOR:

This scene takes place on the edge of a village of poor farmers and in the nearby wilderness, about 20 miles from where the battle will take place.   Around the village stretch fields of winter wheat. Both men and women are working in the field, pulling weeds.
They wear tattered clothes of wool.

VILLAGE MOTHER:
(She screams loudly.)

A LION just took my baby while I was pulling weeds! There it goes with my BABY in its mouth! Everyone come here FAST! We've got to chase it and get my baby back!

FIRST VILLAGE WOMAN:
(She puts her hand over her right eye to block the sun.)

Yes, I see it over there. LISTEN! I hear the baby crying. At least it's not dead yet.

SECOND VILLAGE WOMAN:

I've heard lions often bring home a LIVE baby, so the cubs can practice killing their food.

VILLAGE MOTHER:
(She slaps Second Woman hard.)

Shut UP, you fool! How do you think that makes me feel?
(She starts to cry. Her Husband comes up to her, and puts his arm around her to comfort her.)

HUSBAND:
I wish I could go get our baby, but I wouldn't have a chance against a lioness. Her cubs would probably eat me too.

VILLAGE MOTHER:
(She slaps her husband.)
A lot of help you are.

SECOND VILLAGE WOMAN:
We've got to call LIONGUARD. She's the only one who can get the baby back.

FIRST VILLAGE WOMAN:

Lucky for us, the "Calling Drum" is right over there. I'll pound it hard! Lionguard was here last night, so she's probably near enough to hear it, if I pound it hard like this.

NARRATOR:

She gets a big drum and pounds it several times. In from one side of the stage, Lionguard approaches on a beautiful horse, with a dog running close by. She waves to the villagers as she gets closer.

SECOND VILLAGE WOMAN:

There she is right now. She must have been just behind those hills.

FIRST VILLAGE WOMAN:

Look at how beautiful she is, how STRONG! Her hair's not black like ours; it's almost yellow, like a lion's mane. And her muscles are hard and lean, and look at that BIG bow she's carrying!

HUSBAND:

She LOOKS like a lion, doesn't she? Is that why she's called "Lionguard"?

VILLAGE MOTHER:

(She slaps him again, not so hard.)

No, DUMMY. Haven't you learned any thing about this village you married into?

HUSBAND:

Honey, I've only been here three years!

FIRST VILLAGE WOMAN:

He's got a point. I'll fill him in. She's from the next village over. My cousin lives over there so she told me about her. When Lionguard was young, she only played with boys. Her father would smack her, but she went on doing it behind his back. When she grew up, she hunted with the boys, but she never had sex with them from what I heard.

SECOND VILAGE WOMAN:
And I heard she was a damn good hunter! When the last lionguard was killed, he was a man of course, they gave HER the job. She's been working for several years now, protecting us from the lions. If we didn't have her, the lions would come right into our village to eat our kids, like they used to do.

VILLAGE MOTHER:
(She bows low to Lionguard when she rides up.)

Lionguard, a lioness grabbed my baby and carried it in that direction.

LIONGUARD:
I'll get it back for you if I can. There's no time to waste. Goodbye!

The teacher should say this now: "The people of the village should go back to their seats. LIONGUARD, QUEEN SAPPHO ,and LYDIA should now be center stage. SERGEANT, NURSE, FIRST WOMAN (in the LL), SECOND WOMAN(in the LL) should be stage left. Also there in the Lesbian Legion are LYDIA'S FRIEND, FIRST GIRL, and OTHER NURSE."

NARRATOR:
She rides off towards center stage, with her dog beside her. The villagers leave the stage area. At the right is the Lesbian Legion, but they stay way back from Lionguard for now.

Suddenly in the center area, a lioness appears holding a baby in her mouth. She eats the baby in a few bites, sniffs the air, looks around ,then she roars. *(The Narrator should make several loud lion roars.)*
Lionguard rides up to the lioness, who roars again, and raises up a large paw with claws out. The big cat then leaps up and slashes, first cutting Lionguard in the leg, then ripping open the throat of the horse. The horse wobbles, Lionguard gets off safely, but the horse goes down, bleeding profusely, then dead. Lionguard gets out her short spear then she stabs the lion in the back. Her dog joins the

fight, grabbing at the lioness's neck. The lioness uses her sharp claws to slash at the dog. The dog goes down, wounded badly.

Furious that her dog is hurt, she stabs the lioness hard in the heart. It falls down on its side, then dies.

Lionguard kneels down and puts her arms around her dog. She rips off a piece of her clothes to make a bandage which she puts on the dog, crying as she does it. She ignores her own bleeding leg.

Meanwhile Queen Sappho and Lydia ride up, but Lionguard has been too busy to notice. The rest of the women warriors stay behind them.

QUEEN SAPHOO:
(She looks closely at Lionguard and clearly is impressed. She stays on her horse.)

That was quite a kill, Young Woman; I'm not sure that I could do that now. When I was young, I killed a lion, but it wasn't as big as this one is. Clearly, you know how to use that strong body of yours. You look hard as a rock.

LYDIA:
(She gets off of her horse and goes to the wounded dog.)

May I try to help your dog? I've got a little bag of herbs here around my neck, that I use to stop the flow of blood. Your dog needs some fast. May I touch her?

LIONGUARD:
(She's still on the ground because of her wound. She looks up at Queen Sappho and sort of frowns, then she looks at Lydia and smiles a little.)

Sure you can. I can tell you know how to help her. Please do all you can.

LYDIA:

(She crushes some of the herbs with her hands, takes off the bandage, and puts the herbs on the wound, and then puts the bandage on again.)

That should stop the bleeding for now, but of course the dog can't walk.
(She turns to Queen Sappho and says....)
We have to bring the dog back to our camp. I'll carry her on my horse.
(Lydia puts the dog in a sort of blanket she gets from her saddle bag and then she gets on her horse. Lionguard kisses her dog on the face.)

QUEEN SAPPHO:

You can ride up here with me, Lion Killer.

LIONGUARD:

(Her face looks unsure but interested as well.)

Actually, my name is LionGUARD. Who are you, Honored Old One?

QUEEN SAPPHO:

(She laughs a little.)

Well, I'm not THAT old!   I'm Queen Sappho the Tenth, leader of the Lesbian Legion. This is Lydia, my young helper.

LYDIA:

We better be getting back to the Legion now. The dog needs some other herbs I have back there. And Lionguard, your leg is bleeding quite a bit. You'll need one of our professional nurses so your wound heals clean. You don't want to loose the use of your leg I'm sure.

(They ride over to where the rest of the Lesbian Legion is, then they dismount.)

SERGEANT:

Well, Queen, have you brought us a new recruit? With those broad shoulders, she looks like she's just the type we need.

QUEEN SAPPHO:

Yes, she does look like one of us already, doesn't she? But she's hurt. NURSE, we need you here at once. Where the HELL is that nurse? She's never here when I need her. The new recruit's hurt in the leg pretty bad from what I can see. Now, let me have a closer look.
(The queen goes to Lionguard and then holds Lionguard's leg up in the air, inspecting it. She also slides her hands over Lionguard in a way that is supposed to look medical but isn't really. Lionguard looks ill at ease but puts up with it.)

LYDIA:
(She speaks in a firm, commanding voice.)

WOMEN WARRIORS, let's get to work! Each of you take your shirts off so you don't ruin your uniforms. Do the jobs you always do each time we make a new camp. We have to meet up with Alexander's army tomorrow, so we don't have time to waste.

SERGEANT:
(She takes off her shirt then turns to address the rest of the women. They take their shirts off too.)

Yes, Ma'am. Let's get to work. You women put the tent poles up, so we'll have a nice place for our party. You girls over there, go get the canvas ready to make a roof for us. The rest of you, get out the kitchen utensils and start to cook for the feast tonight. We want a lot of good food for our last feast before the battle.

(First Woman and Second Woman nod yes. Both go off by themselves. They unpack metal cooking things, then set them up, light a fire, and start making food.)

FIRST WOMAN:
I'm really in the mood to cook today! Now what're we going to make?

SECOND WOMAN:

Me too. Well, let me think. My mother taught me how to make a pudding with those berries I see over there.

FIRST WOMAN:

Lucky we got a barrel of honey in the last village. I like my pudding really sweet.
(In comes Nurse, looking worried.)

NURSE:

 Sorry I'm late. One of the new women just started her period and she was having a lot of pain.   Now what can I do here?

QUEEN SAPPHO:

This is our new recruit, Lionguard. She's been slashed on her thigh there. Get her fixed up fast because we'll need her in the battle tomorrow.

LIONGUARD:

Please help my dog first. The pretty one put some herbs on her wound, but she said some other herbs were needed too.

LYDIA:

Yes, I put on aloe vera and willow leaves, but I think the dog needs some feverfew too. Don't you?

NURSE:

I have some here in my bag. Help me hold the dog while I take off the old bandage and put on a new one.

LIONGUARD:

Please take good care of her. She's been my ONLY friend for years. I've always felt alone, except for her. I thought I was the only one like me.
(She then looks up from her dog and looks around to see all the women

around her. She now speaks in a soft voice,talking to herself.)

But maybe things are different here. All these strong, proud women everywhere, and they seem to like me too. What a great feeling! It's like I'm HOME at last.

LYDIA:
Sappho, we better be moving on. We have to go over our battle strategy. I see the other leaders are already talking over there. Let's join them now, or they'll make decisions without us.

QUEEN SAPPHO:

You're right. I wish this Legion weren't an ELECTED monarchy. I may be the queen, but most of the women warriors always seem to want to do things their own way. I HATE those women's council meetings we have to have. Yes, let's get over there so they can see who's the boss.
       (She turns to talk to Nurse and Lionguard.)
Nurse, do the best you can with your two new patients. I'll see you, Lionguard, at the dinner tonight. You can sit right next to me!

LYDIA:
(She smiles warmly at Lionguard.)
I hope I get some time with you too. I 'd really like to hear the story of your life.

NARRATOR:
The Queen and Lydia leave. Nurse finishes with the dog and now examines the thigh of Lionguard. Nurse crushes seeds and puts them into hot water to make a calming drink which she gets Lionguard to drink. Nurse and Lionguard have a long talk while Nurse stitches up the wound on Lionguard's leg, and then she takes off the old clothing and massages Lionguard slowly and smoothly.
The dog stays asleep.

NURSE:

Let me slip that old robe off of you; it's full of bugs. I need to give you a massage. It'll calm you down and get your energy flowing again.

My, my, but you have a BEAUTIFUL body: you're soft and round and smooth, but so well-muscled too. I can see why the Queen wants you to sit next to her! But, Honey, be careful with your heart. The Queen doesn't want anyone for long.

LIONGUARD:

I'm not sure what you mean. My heart?

NURSE:

Forget I said that. I just don't want to see you hurt.

LIONGUARD:

(She looks unsure, puzzled.)

Why would she hurt me? I'm on her side. I don't really understand what's going on with you women. Would you please tell me more about this Lesbian Legion?   And what's a "lesbian" anyway?

NURSE:

A lesbian is a person from the island of LESBOS, a rather small island in the Mediterranean Sea, several hundred miles from here. Long ago a woman named SAPPHO was born there. Her father was a teacher and she was his only child, so he taught her to read and write. Soon she was making poems that people said were the most beautiful short poems ever written. Many of her poems were about friendships between women. She wrote about her feelings for the girls she loved.

She got so famous that Athens and all the other Greek cities started to send her the young women who were smart and were not interested in having children. Sappho began a sort of college for them, a place where women would be free to be whatever they wanted to be. Everyone loved the scholarship and the sex.

LIONGUARD:
You mean the women had sex with each other?

NURSE:
Yes, they did. They just did whatever they wanted to do, and some of them found they really enjoyed making love with other women. This kind of sex became so popular on our island of Lesbos, that other Greeks began to call it "lesbian", after our island's name.

LIONGUARD:

So you women all are lesbians, in both meanings of the word?

NURSE:
Well, most of us are. Some of the woman were born in other parts of the Greek world, like in Athens say, but they all came to Lesbos to study with in Sappho's college, so we're all called lesbians.

LIONGUARD:
And you all have sex with each other?

NURSE:
(She laughs pleasantly.)

Well, not all of us at once of course---we leave that to Greek MEN! But we do make love in whatever way we feel like. Most of us find one woman we like best of all, so we become a couple. We're faithful to our partners, at least most of the time, and we often fight in battle right next to our partner. It makes us fierce!

LIONGUARD:

That leads to another question. How did you lesbians get to have your own army?

NURSE:

That's a long story. At first when the graduates from Sappho's college left, they couldn't find a job. They didn't want to be wives or prostitutes, which were women's only choices. Also they tended to be physically strong women, women who liked to play sports.

Then Sappho got an idea. Almost all upper class men were soldiers, so why couldn't her girls be soldiers too? She knew that most men have more muscle strength than most women, so our girls wouldn't do very well in hand to hand fighting. Then she remembered how most girls love horses and most women have better fine motor skills than most men, so she bought lots of horses and hired men to teach the girls how to use bows and arrows. Our young women learned fast and well. In a short time we had a new thing, a brand new thing on earth---WOMEN WARRIORS!

Since most countries HIRE many of their soldiers, we looked around for a country that would pay our women to fight for them. The Greek island of Rhodes was the first to hire us. Our mounted archers did so well in that war, that we got famous. Many countries wanted us to work for them because our soldiers were such good riders, and they shot their arrows very accurately. We named ourselves the LESBIAN LEGION. Our motto is WOMEN WARRIORS RULE!

Sorry I got so long-winded.   I guess all this matters a lot to me.

LIONGUARD:
I can see why. It's a great story. It's what I always wanted, but never thought could be. I'm already a woman warrior. I guess all I have to do now is--- have SEX with one of you!

NURSE:
(She laughs.)
Well, you don't exactly HAVE to have sex, but from what I've seen since you've been here, I think you WILL soon. The Queen obviously has sexual plans for you, and I'm fairly sure young Lydia does too.

LIONGUARD:
You really think so? The QUEEN, the number one woman, she wants ME? And that beautiful Lydia---she does too? I can hardly believe it! It sort of scares me, but it thrills me too!

NURSE:

I'm done with your massage now. What you need right now is REST. Why don't you and your dog just sleep right here for the afternoon. I'll come and wake you up at sundown so you'll have time to get ready for the pre-battle feast.

NARRATOR:

Nurse leaves this area while Lionguard and her dog sleep. Several hours pass. The women finish putting up the big tent and the cooking too. Then nurse goes to where Lionguard is still sleeping and puts a hand on her to wake her up. Hearing this, the dog wakes up and starts to rub her leg. Lionguard gets down on the floor to play with the dog and talk softly to her.

LIONGUARD:

You're a whole lot better now, aren't you, Girl? I was afraid I'd lost you but here you are as sweet as ever.

(She keeps on petting the dog who smiles and keeps rubbing on her. When this happens, Lionguard winces in pain.)

Go easy on that leg, Sweetheart. I'm a lot better too, but I'm still tender there. These women here are something else, aren't they? They've practically cured you and me! And I have so much else to tell you. These women all have sex with women, and they're professional soldiers. What do you think of that? Should we stay here and try out this life a while?

(The dog sort of moves her head as if saying yes.)

That's what I think too. I think we should give this idea a chance. If we don't like it, we can always go away, can't we?

NURSE:

(She's smiling,and she is carrying a lion skin made into a sexy dress, which she hands to Lionguard.)
Stand up for me, Dear, so I can see if your new dress fits. The Queen had it made for you---from the skin of the lion you killed this morning.

LIONGUARD:

Things have changed SO fast. My life will never be the same, will it?

NURSE:

I suppose not, Dear. And wait until you have sex! It'll blow your mind away. It's MUCH better than it is with men.

LIONGUARD:

Well I've never been with a man either. I guess I have a lot to learn!

NURSE:

We'll start with how to dress. Let's take this thing off your hair and let it fall down. By the mother goddess, you look SO beautiful. That long, blond hair flows over your shoulders like a cascade of precious gold.

Now put on this dress. Let me arrange your breasts right. There we go. They almost spill out of the dress, but not quite---just the way they should. The color of this lion skin fits you perfectly, and the length is right too. You truly are the Greek goddess, great DIANA OF THE HUNT. You're her in the flesh! Like Diana, you've never known a man, nor wanted to. Like her, you hunt where ever you choose. You're wild, and chaste, and free!

LIONGUARD:

I feel DIFFERENT, that's for sure. More powerful and more womanly ----BOTH! *(She looks down and pets her dog who is looking at her in wonder.)*
Say, Sweetheart, what do you think of your old mother now?
(The dog barks several times and both women laugh.)

I guess she thinks I'm someone new.

NURSE:
You are! Now let's take you to the dinner. We're eating over there.
(They walk over to where all the other women are.)

NARRATOR:
Queen Sappho, Lydia, Lydia's Friend, First Woman, Second Woman, First Girl, Nurse, and Other Nurse are sitting around a big campfire singing. When the Queen sees Lionguard and Nurse, she makes the "come here" signal with her hands. They come to her and both bow. The Queen gets up and gives Lionguard a big and prolonged hug.

QUEEN SAPHHO:
 You feel as good as you look! And you look like a goddess! All that golden hair! You look like Athena, the warrior goddess of Athens. Come sit right by me. Nurse, go over there and sit with the other FEMS. I'll take care of this one from now on!

(She signals "go away" with her hand to First Girl who was sitting there. First Girl stands up and bows, then she starts to cry.)

FIRST GIRL:
(She sobs some as she talks.)

I didn't last long, but I see why. How could I compare to this golden woman? I'm nowhere near as good as she is.

FIRST WOMAN:
(She stands up to hug First Girl and pats her on the back and smooths her hair.)

Don't cry, Dear. You're plenty good enough. You're so good with your bow that your arrows hit the mark every time.

FIRST GIRL:
(She stops crying now.)
Well, not EVERY time, but most of the time, if I do say so myself.

SECOND WOMAN:
That a girl. Be proud of who you are. With us warrior women, a good shot counts for more than golden hair.

FIRST WOMAN:
Let's get away from the fire; it's too hot this close. Let's go over there, by those trees. I want to tell you about a new way to make a bow I just found out about. *(They exit.)*

NURSE:
(On the other side of the campfire, the two nurses talk in quiet voices.)
I don't like the way she calls us "FEMS" and sneers as she says it. It's like she thinks were second class lesbians.

OTHER NURSE:
It seems to me that she hasn't learned yet that masculine and feminine are the two ends of a long spectrum. Each of us has her own place on the spectrum. We shouldn't worry about being masculine or feminine; we should just be who we are. No one is better or worse, no matter what the old queen says.

NURSE:
(She whispers again.)
I'm starting to think it's time to get rid of her. We need to pick a new queen, a more open-minded person, a person who knows how complex a woman's sexuality really is.

OTHER NURSE:
(She reaches for a wine jug and pours for herself and for Nurse a cup that they drink right away.)

I think you're probably right but enough talk for now. I'm ready for a good drink, aren't you?
(They drink their wine. The "spotlight" goes to another part of the campfire circle.)

(Lydia's Friend almost whispers to Lydia, but Lydia speaks in a proud, firm voice.)

LYDIA'S FRIEND:
The Queen's CRUEL sometimes. She didn't even think about that poor girl's feelings. And several times she told me I was a fool, in front of my friends worse yet.

LYDIA:
You're absolutely right. Sappho's starting to go too far. In our Lesbian Legion, the Queen is supposed to be just a first among equals. She's NOT supposed to be like the Persian King of Kings, who does what ever he wants to do. She's ELECTED after all. We chose her to lead. We're progressive Greeks. We believe in democracy, at least to some degree. We know that the INDIVIDUAL is what really counts.

LYDIA'S FRIEND:
Another thing that makes me agree with you is how she always has her favorites. They may come and go, but there are always those she likes a lot, and then the rest of us.   That's not the equality that the Lesbian Legion is supposed to represent.

LYDIA:
I'm starting to think that we have to do something about this problem RIGHT NOW. As the second in command, I have the right to call for a meeting of the All Women's Council , and I think I'll do it. What do you think?

LYDIA'S FRIEND:
Why not? Everyone's here and nobody's drunk yet. I'm sick and tired of how unfair she is. I'll bet most of the others are too.

NARRATOR:
Lydia stands up, and speaks in a loud, public voice to get the attention of everyone. When the others see Lydia standing, they quit their eating and drinking and look at her, because they know she's a good leader.

LYDIA:
Women Warriors, I have something important to say. I hereby call us into session as the All Women's Council. As you know, when we're

acting in this way, we all get a chance to vote on some important issue.

QUEEN SAPPHO:
(She stands up at once and looks with anger at Lydia.)

How DARE you, young woman! Who do you think you are?
I was elected Queen----not YOU!   Sit down at once, you fool!

NURSE:
(She stands up and speaks in a firm voice.)

She has a RIGHT to call the All Women's Council into session and we all know that's true. YOU sit down, Sappho!

OTHER NURSE:
What's on your mind, Lydia?

LYDIA:
I propose that we ask this Sappho to STEP DOWN as queen. It's time to elect a new Sappho for us.
(Many of the women looked surprised, some open their mouths in shock.)

LYDIA'S FRIEND:
This Sappho's done a lot that's wrong. Look at how she's practically forced Lionguard to be with her, and we know she's done that to many others too.

LYDIA:
She favors certain people, which makes the rest of us feel left out. She also criticizes people in front of other people. She doesn't care about our feelings at all.

NURSE:
She calls us "FEMS" and says it with a sneer.

OTHER NURSE:
She thinks we all should be just like her!

FIRST GIRL:
She broke my heart.

QUEEN SAPPHO:
(Of course she's furious by now. She shakes both fists in rage.)

You silly bitches, you don't know what you're talking about!
Everything I do, I do for you. Without my leadership, we wouldn't be
where we are. We're about to fight along side of the greatest general
since the world began. That's all because of ME!

LYDIA:
(In a calm, strong, in control sort of voice)

You see what I mean now, don't you? She's an egomaniac. She
doesn't care about us at all. Let's vote her OUT.
     Please raise your hand if you vote to get rid of this Sappho now.

(Almost all the hands go up.)

Then you're DONE ; you're no longer our Sappho. Please leave at
once.

LYDIA'S FRIEND:
(In a proud, happy voice)

That leaves YOU in charge now, Lydia.   Women Warriors, raise your
hands if you want Lydia as our new Sappho.

(Almost all the hands go up. Many people start to clap and cheer.)

LYDIA:
(She looks pleased of course but she wants to get on with it too.)

Thank you, my friends! I'll do my best to make you glad that you've
chosen me. Now let's finish our food and get to bed. Tomorrow we'll
meet with Alexander the Great. We'll show him how STRONG Women
Warriors are!

SCENE EIGHT---------"HEROES AND HELL"

MARCH 24, 333 B.C.

CHARACTERS:

ALEXANDER
HEPHAISTON
QUEEN MOTHER SISYGAMBIS
FOUR ROYAL GIRLS
FIRST SOLDIER
NURSE
FIRST NARRATOR
SECOND NARRATOR

Teacher please say this: " I need the following characters to come up here to the stage area.   Only FIRST NARRATOR, SECOND NARRATOR, ALEXANDER, and HEPHAISTON."

HEPHAISTON:
They're the FIERCEST men on earth, and they LOVE you, Alexander!

ALEXANDER:
No more than I love THEM.
I must speak to them now.

FIRST NARRATOR:

He rides up and down the battle line. He calls many of them by name.
He remembers things about their lives: who's been wounded before,
where they're from, what nicknames they are called. From his horse
he calls to them, with a voice high and clear, like a ringing bell.

ALEXANDER:
I'm in YOU and you're in ME.
Alexander and his men are ONE.
Men, say it after me now!

EVERYONE:
(Every one in the room says this, all together, loudly.)

I'm in you and you're in me.
Alexander and his men are ONE.

ALEXANDER:
This is our day, men. We've trained for it all our lives! WAR's the ultimate sport; it's what makes us men!
COMPETITION is who we are. We want to beat the rest.
That's why we're here today. We'll out fight them in EVERY single way!

FIRST NARRATOR:
All the men on Alexander's army cheer. Twenty thousand soldiers raise their right hands in fists in the air as they cheer. Over and over the whole army shouts, "ALEXANDER! ALEXANDER! ALEXANDER!"

ALEXANDER:
(Suddenly he frowns deeply. He speaks to Hephaiston in a sad, quiet voice.)

When I talk like that, it scares me sometimes. I sound like a HOWLING wolf. What if fighting's WRONG? In my mind, I see all those who'll die soon. All because of me. Am I a HOUND OF HELL?

HEPHAISTON:
(He puts his arm around Alexander protectively.)

You always have these thoughts before a battle and maybe it IS time for us to reconsider war. Maybe war's not the supreme sport we've always thought, but we'll talk about that later. We can't turn back now, can we?

ALEXANDER:
(He puts a big smile back on his face.)

You're right of course; we can't turn back. Besides I don't really

WANT us to. I want to be famous as the greatest warrior since the world began. This is how I build my fame!

(The cheering has ended now so Alexander puts his hands on both sides of his mouth, so he can be heard at a distance.)

Friends, these are my commands! I want all you infantry men to get into your phalanx formations, fifty men wide and fifty men long. You in the front two rows of each phalanx, take both hands and hold your twelve foot spears out in front of you. You in the middle hold your spears up in the air to keep arrows away. The rest of you be in reserve to take the places of any of your friends who are killed. The enemy will think each phalanx is a giant hedgehog of spears. If you each do your job, you'll be INVINCIBLE, twenty thousand men of iron!

    I want you cavalry men to mount your horses now. I can see they're ready to run. I myself will lead you like I always do. Get your long lances out. When I give the signal call, follow me. You'll be able to tell it's me by my white feathered helmet. Follow me in close formation. We'll be a moving wall of horse!

    Now, Stallion, get your Leathermen in their chariots at once. MOUNT UP, LEATHERMEN! Stallion, lead your men to the far left of the field, then hide them as much as possible behind the small forest over there. Keep them out of sight until you hear the horn blow, then gallup fast towards me. Get behind the enemy if you can. I'll pound them from one side, and you get them in the rear. You men can do that well I'm sure!

    That's it, men. Do what I just said NOW. We're taking the defense, so all we have to do is wait for them to attack. Let them come to us. That way they'll wear themselves out right away. All we have to do is stand here HARD. We can do that well, can't we?

ALL ALEXANDER'S MEN:
(They say this all together.)

We'll stand here HARD, Alexander. We'll stand here hard FOR YOU!

FIRST NARRATOR:

The battle begins. King Darius, standing in his large chariot plated with gold, is surrounded by many messengers who take his orders to his men and return with information about what's happening. He says to the messengers, "My foot soldiers with their short spears should start marching to the enemy lines. If they are killed by Alexander's phalanx formations, I order the next row to advance. If they die, the next,and then the next. I have ten times as many men so we can keep this up until the Greeks surrender."

SECOND NARRATOR:

But the Greek phalanx formations keep killing each line of attacking Persians; nevertheless, the Persians keep on coming, row after row. Dead Persian bodies pile up but the new rows climb over them and keep up their attack.

FIRST NARRATOR:

King Darius then sends in his horse soldiers, his knights with swords. Seeing this, Alexander himself leads his mounted warriors out to fight the Persians. Alexander fights fiercely from his horse, killing several Persians. All the Greeks fight furiously, but they are hugely outnumbered.

SECOND NARRATOR:

Alexander now blows a trumpet a servant brings him. At its sound, the Leathermen of Thrace ride in on black chariots from where they had been hiding. The top man on each chariot turns left and right, killing with his spear, while the bottom man keeps the horses moving fast. The Persian cavalry fights hard, with the Greeks on one side and with their friends the Leathermen on the other side.

FIRST NARRATOR:

Hearing about this, King Darius sends in two thousand Persian chariots. Alexander's side is now outnumbered but the fight seems about even, and then Darius sends in his secret weapons: first camels ridden by men with bows and arrows, and then---ELEPHANTS, each making an awful noise. Each giant elephant has a man riding him who has a bow and arrows.

SECOND NARRATOR:

Never having seen or heard elephants, some of the horses on Alexander's side panic, causing the Leathermen chariots to smash into each other. The panic spreads like wildfire with horses and then men going crazy with fear. CHAOS explodes everywhere. Alexander rides from place to place, bringing some order where he is, but chaos, like wildfire, breaks out again as soon as he moves on. DISASTER looms!

FIRST NARRATOR:

Hephaiston also tries to get the men and chariots back under control, but without success. From some distance, he looks at Alexander then raises his hands in the air, signaling "what else can we do"?

SECOND NARRATOR:

Then suddenly Alexander puts his right hand to his ear: in the distance he hears a sound only made by the special horns of the LESBIAN LEGION. His face turns from frown to joy---HELP is on the way!

FIRST NARRATOR:

The Lesbian Legion has come up BEHIND the Persian army. At full gallup, up they ride, their trumpets blaring ----- a mighty WAVE of WOMEN WARRIORS, shooting arrows fast and true! As they get near, the exhausted Persians throw down their weapons. Thousands turn and run away.

SECOND NARRATOR:

Seeing his army dissolve before his eyes, King Darius rushes to say goodbye to his mother, then he jumps onto a special chariot he had made to be the fastest one on earth. His driver speeds away, pushing through the fleeing troops. The King of Kings has run away!

Teacher, please say at this point,"I want ALEXANDER AND HEPHAISTON to come up here."

FIRST NARRATOR:

On the other side of the room, Alexander and Hephaiston ride in, covered with blood. Hephaiston's right arm hangs limp because it's badly hurt. Alexander has a wound on his arm and on one of his mighty thighs.

ALEXANDER:

(He points to a place in the distance.)
NO! NO! OH, NO-O-O-O! He's getting away! King Darius is trying to get AWAY!

HEPHAISTON:

Yes, I see his golden chariot right over there. I see his mother's tent. Look, he's saying good-bye to her. He's getting out of his gold chariot and getting into a black chariot that's pulled by EIGHT horses. He's pulling out fast. That shit is RUNNING AWAY!

ALEXANDER:

(His voice shows that he's almost crazy with rage.)

It CAN'T be true! I'm the favorite of the gods; they wouldn't do this to me. This just CAN'T be true! What a COWARD! He's getting tired so he just runs away. He's leaving his army, he's leaving his mother. That fool is GETTING AWAY!

(He's so disappointed and so mad he shakes his fists at the sky and at the direction Darius has gone.)

You goddamn son of a bitch, you CHEATED me, you shit!

HEPHAISTON:
And we'll never catch up with him. That eight horse chariot is the fastest thing on earth. I've heard people say that a lot. He's fucking GONE!

ALEXANDER:
(He clinches his teeth and makes fists with both hands, then he calms down fast.)
I HAVE to get myself under control. I HAVE to let him go for now. I have to concentrate on what I need to do here. Now what was it? Oh, I remember. I need to go talk with King Darius's mother, with Sisygambis. I've been writing to her for a month now. I want to meet her face to face.

HEPHAISTON:
(His face shows extreme shock.)

You've been WRITING to a Persian Queen! Why in the world would you do that?

ALEXANDER:

My Persian Boy told me that she has known for quite a while that we'd win, and she's glad about it. She thinks her son is a poor leader. She thinks I'll do a much better job for her people. So I wrote to her about a plan I had in mind.

HEPHAISTON:
What plan is that?

ALEXANDER:
(His face lights up and he smiles as he thinks about his plan.)

I want to UNITE our two peoples! I want our men to marry their women, so we can all become ONE! Our Greek idea of individual freedom will be joined to their idea that the group comes first. We'll have the best of both worlds, and we could have UNIVERSAL PEACE.

HEPHAISTON:
(His face shows amazement and then he quickly warms up to the idea.)

My god, Alexander, that's AMAZING! That's bold--- even for YOU.
That may be the best idea you've EVER had!

ALEXANDER:
(He smiles a big smile then gives his mate a hug.)

I'm really glad you like it; I was afraid you might not.
But we need to get to Sisygambis at once. She promised she would
take care of the Persian side of my idea.   She also said she'd help me
with the Persian surrender, so her people can see I mean them only
good.

HEPHAISTON:

Let's find her now. Royal Women always use a silver tent, don't they?

ALEXANDER:

Yes, they do. There it is!   Let's ride over there now.
 Teacher, please say: "I need Queen Mother SISYGAMBIS to come here
 now to the stage area. Also I need the four ROYAL GIRLS."

SECOND NARRATOR:
At one side of the stage is Sisygambis and with her are the four Royal
Girls. Alexander and Hephaiston dismount and enter the silver tent.

FIRST NARRATOR:
Sisygambis, the Queen Mother of Persia, is a dignified and still
beautiful woman eighty years old. She, like most Persians, is quite
tall. She's dressed in a flowing silver gown, like they wear at the
Academy Awards, with diamond jewelry on her head and neck. Her
four granddaughters are in their late teens. They are all dressed in
pink silk. All of them have a transparent, white silk veil over their
faces.

Alexander and Hephaiston have washed off the blood that has covered them. Both have bandages on. Hephaiston, several inches taller than Alexander, has put on a new military cloak of red, but Alexander is still wearing the cloak he wore in the battle, full of rips, almost shredded.

SECOND NARRATOR:
When they enter, both bow very low to her. Then Sisygambis slowly walks up to them, looks at both men, and then kneels down at the feet of........HEPHAISTON! She puts her hands in front of her, palms up, in a pleading position. Several servants in the room look horrified and gasp.
  Then Alexander puts out his hand to touch hers and he helps her stand up. He smiles a warm smile as he looks at her.

ALEXANDER:
(He talks slowly, as if saying something very important.)

MOTHER, you are not wrong.   HE TOO is Alexander!

SISYGAMBIS:
(She adjusts to her mistake easily and then puts her hand on Alexander's cheek,tenderly.)
My new son, I am glad that you are here. You indeed look like a King of Kings, however short you are. You will do better than my real son. I can see it in your face.

ALEXANDER:
(He bows again and smiles his biggest smile.)

Thank you, Mother. I think that you will be the GOOD mother that I have always wanted. I see THAT in your face!

SISYGAMBIS:
(She's goes back to business fast.)

Dear Boy, I have done as I said I would. Many of our highest leaders are already pledged to you, and the rest will follow soon because of my son's cowardly behavior. The transition to your rule will be smooth.

And I have many young women ready to marry whomever you pick from your side.

(She beckons to First Royal Girl, who comes up to Sisygambis and kneels at her feet. Sisygambis reaches down to lift the girl's veil.)

You see, dear Boy, how fair she is . This one here, Darius's oldest daughter, is for you, if you wish.

(Alexander looks less than pleased,and Hephaiston looks furious.)

ALEXANDER:
(He puts his arm around Hephaiston, who looks relieved by this gesture.)

Mother dear, we will decide about that later.   My MATE and I must go now. We want to check on the wounded soldiers. We have nurses ready to help them.

SISYGAMBIS:
Will they help my Persian boys too?

ALEXANDER:
(He smiles and takes her hand into his.)
Of course they will. Our boys and yours are ONE now. We'll start that right away.

Teacher please say, " I want all the Persian women to return to their seats. I want FIRST SOLDIER and NURSE to come up here now. ALEXANDER and HEPHAISTON remain."

FIRST NARRATOR:
He bows low to her, then he and his mate walk away. They go over to the other side of the stage where the dead and dying are moaning in a terrible, heart-breaking way. In every direction dead bodies of horses and of men stretch into the distance. Blood is everywhere. It's a scene from Hell.

ALEXANDER:
   (He comes up to First Soldier who is bleeding profusely from a head wound. He kneels down and takes the dying soldier's hand in his.)

NURSE, get over here at once! This man needs your help.
(Alexander uses his own cloak to try to stop the blood that's flowing from the wound. He speaks in a soft, caring voice to the soldier.)
   Sweet boy, please don't move like that. Stay still. A nurse is on the way. I'm here with you. You're safe. Your king is with you now.
(Alexander kisses First Soldier on the cheek.)

FIRST SOLDIER:
 I did my best, Sir. I fought hard for you.

ALEXANDER:
 (He is crying now but trying to hide it from the dying soldier.)

Of COURSE you did, brave boy. You're my HERO. You risked your life for me.

(Nurse comes up, looks quickly at the big wound, then shakes his head no, meaning he doesn't have a chance to live. Nurse gives the dying boy a big drink from a bottle of tincture of opium.)

NURSE :
Soldier, drink this now. It'll make you feel much better.

FIRST SOLDIER:
(Immediately high from the drug, he boldly reaches up to touch Alexander on the cheek.)

I see DEATH coming for me, Sir. Even you can't conquer him.
(His hand comes down as his head goes back. He has obviously left this world.)

ALEXANDER:
(He raises both hands up in the air, almost crazy with grief. Hephaiston puts his arm around him.)

NO! I CAN'T! I can't conquer Death. All I do is feed his HUNGRY MOUTH! I'm just a servant that brings Death more to eat.

FIRST NARRATOR:

He's getting even more out of control. He's very near insanity. He uses his right arm to make Hephaiston look all around the battle field, then he points at different parts of the battlefield , one by one.

ALEXANDER:

Look around you. Do you see that pile of bodies? Look there, and there, and there. That HILL of bodies! That MOUNTAIN of death! I've made this place..... a red LANDSCAPE of Hell.

And it's all MY FAULT. I started this war. I brought them here to die.

And what FOR? The Greek Idea? That's BULLSHIT! I did it for MYSELF, that's all. I did it for my GLORY. That's my glory---the blood of other men. Where's the glory there? I'm BAD, I'm Evil; I'm the worst MONSTER since the world began.

SECOND NARRATOR:

He starts to cry, to sob, totally out of control. Hephaiston puts his arms around Alexander, who cries on his chest, like a child.

HEPHAISTON:
(He talks in a calm,thoughtful voice.)

You HAVE to get control of yourself, Alexander. People can't see you sob.

But I know what you mean about what we've done. War's no sport; we were wrong. All it does is kill. It's time for us to stop!

After all, we've shown the world we're tough, in the traditional way of men. What if we could excel at something BETTER? What if we tried to build things up, not tear them down?

ALEXANDER:
(He quits crying because he's listening now to his friend's idea.)

And how would we do that? We're warriors--- that's what men do, don't they?

HEPHAISTON:
(His voice gains in positive energy as he talk.)
That always has been, but does it HAVE to be? Maybe there's a better way to be a man. What if our army HELPED people for a change? We could build new houses for them and new roads too. Think of all the GOOD our strong young men could do!

ALEXANDER:
(Now he's smiling. He shakes Hephaiston' s hand,and pats him on the back.)

You're right again, dear friend, you're right again of course. Let's make peace instead of war. We'll make all the nations ONE under my rule. We'll make a new, a better world. Let's start RIGHT NOW!
(He raises his right hand up in the air, as if he were leading a cavalry charge.)

SCENE NINE------------------"WHAT'S NEXT?"

APRIL 24, 333 B.C.

CHARACTERS:

FIRST NARRATOR
SECOND NARRATOR
ALEXANDER
PERSIAN BOY
SISYGAMBIS
HEPHAISTON

Teacher,please say, "Up here in front I need ALEXANDER, PERSIAN BOY, SISYGAMBIS,sitting together talking. HEPHAISTON is back stage ready to come out."

FIRST NARRATOR:

A month has passed. Alexander has moved his army to fabled BABYLON, the richest city on earth. It's located on the Euphrates River in Mesopotamia (now Iraq), the site of the world's first civilizations. The vast age, the endless wealth, the incredible diversity of Babylon make it seem alien to most of his men, but Alexander rejoices in its splendor.

SECOND NARRATOR:

He is sitting in the famous Hanging Gardens of Babylon, sheltered from the blazing sun by sweet-smelling jasmine vines and orchids. Beside him sits the Persian Boy who is now treated as a friend, not as a servant. Both Alexander and his Boy are dressed in gold-embroidered silk robes: Alexander's is royal purple, the Boy's a soft shade of blue. Both have on subtle eye make-up in the style of the Persian court. Near them on a jeweled throne is the Queen Mother Sisygambis, again dressed and veiled entirely in silver and diamonds, like a glittering ghost.

ALEXANDER:

(He puts his arm around the Persian Boy and kisses him on the cheek, then he gives a little laugh. He says in a soft voice.)
Are you in COSTUME?

PERSIAN BOY:

(He gives Alexander a wink and then a little laugh. He speaks in a charming, soft, "feminine" way as usual.)

Aren't we ALWAYS?

ALEXANDER:

(He laughs a little at this inside joke.)
Of course we are. Let's keep that in mind as we do our work today. All the world's a stage!

PERSIAN BOY:
(He speaks now in a formal voice, rather loud, but still very high.)

Great King, I've had another idea!

ALEXANDER:
(Laughing again.)
It's just on time.   It's been exactly an hour since your last!

PERSIAN BOY:
Now be serious---please!
This one is REALLY good. Here it is.   When we have the wedding of you and your officers to royal Persian women---what if we include OTHER sorts of people, people who would also like to be joined together? Wouldn't this express your idea that we all should be proud who we are, and marry who we want? This way we could celebrate both racial and sexual TOLERATION---all at the same time!

ALEXANDER:
(He pats Persian Boy on the back and says sincerely….)

It would indeed, and splendidly, at that. So now I command this: our big wedding will be INCLUSIVE.   I want representatives of EVERY sort of sexuality to share this day with me.

(Alexander suddenly remembers that Queen Sisygambis, who has been snoring a little, is there and she's rather deaf, so he talks loudly.)

Great Queen of the East, remember the idea you had a while back that your royal women should marry my best men? Well, what do you think of including some other people too?   I would pick them out, and I'd only pick outstanding ones of course---people you would be proud to know.

SISYGAMBIS:
What ever you think is best, my son. In the past month, I have learned to trust your judgement in all things. You have such fine ideas!

ALEXANDER:
(He smiles at this because his real mother almost never complimented him.)

Thank you, Mother. I treasure your opinion. But this idea isn't mine. My Persian Boy right here---he had this idea.

SISYGAMBIS:

Since I discovered that he comes from an old noble family, I have learned to take him more seriously.
(Now she looks closely at Persian Boy.)
My boy, that is an excellent idea you have had. I approve of any thing we can do to help the arrogant Greeks become more tolerant.

ALEXANDER:
Then what do you think of THIS idea, Mother? It came to me in a dream last night. What if I ask all the Persian noble families to lend me their best boys for a time? We'll start a school for them where they'll learn to speak perfect Greek, and where they'll learn to fight like us. Also we'll expect them to teach their teachers how to speak Persian, so we can build mutual understanding. Everyone will win!

PERSIAN BOY:
(He looks at Alexander with total, worshipping love.)

That's a WONDERFUL idea, Alexander! It'll be another step to bring our two worlds together.

ALEXANDER:
Speaking of that, let's make a list right now of the people we'll invite to be in our inclusive wedding. First of all, there'll be Hephaiston and I who will be marrying two daughters of King Darius, then some of my top men who will marry the other Persian royal girls that you've picked out for them, Sisygambis.

PERSIAN BOY:
(*His voice is full of excitement and positive energy.*)

Let's invite the Stallion, the leader of the Leathermen. I've heard that he and that smart boy of his have fallen in love. Imagine HIM in love!

ALEXANDER:
(*He laughs at the idea.*)

I admit it's hard to do, but I've heard that too! I certainly owe him for the help his horsemen gave us at the battle. Yes, the Stallion for sure. Who else?

PERSIAN BOY:

How about your common soldiers? You owe them most of all. Why don't we pick out two of those big, hairy men who love each other, and ask them to be in the wedding?

ALEXANDER:
Of course we should. They deserve all the honor they can get.
Say, what about the women? We've got to have two from the Lesbian Legion. I've noticed their new leader, Lydia, really seems to like that blond recruit a lot. Let's have them be married with the rest of us.

PERSIAN BOY:
Then there's those two mountain women that helped you find the path that helped us win. Didn't you say they were very much in love? Let's honor them this way! Have them bring their son too.

ALEXANDER:
Of course! I like all this very much. I'll send out messengers at once to invite all of our inclusive guests. This is going to be a brand new thing, a wedding that the world will never forget.

SISYGAMBIS:
(*Suddenly she seems quite alert. She joins the conversation easily, having missed very little.*)

If you really want diversity, what about the TRANSGENDERED one that my son Darius trusted so much? I find him quite intelligent and pleasant to be with. He told me once that he's lonely---that he wants a good man to build a life with. Why don't we find him a man that's willing and have them get married too?

PERSIAN BOY:
(He bows his head very low. His voice is the sort you use when talking to the big boss.)

Great Queen, I am deeply aware of the honor your presence does to me, your unworthy servant. May I please make a reply to what Your Majesty just said?

SISYGAMBIS:
Of course. We are talking here informally after all. Please tell me what you are thinking.

PERSIAN BOY:
I'm thinking that Your Majesty is truly open-minded. You will be the FIRST CITIZEN of our new, united world.

SISYGAMBIS:
(At first she is serious like she usually is but by the end of the speech she is smiling her fullest smile.)
Thank you. Now there's one more thing I want to say.
I wonder if there's a man out there for ME?

(Alexander and Persian Boy look shocked ,and then start to laugh with her at the joke.)

ALEXANDER:
Dear Lady, what man could be GOOD enough for you?

SISYGAMBIS:
(She still is smiling so it's not clear if she's being serious or not.)

Perhaps I need a WOMAN.

ALEXANDER:
Perhaps you do! If only you had a twin; only another YOU could equal you, in wisdom and in wit!

(All three of them are laughing in good cheer, when Hephaiston walks in. He frowns deeply when he sees Persian Boy.)

HEPHAISTON:
(He speaks in a sarcastic, bitter way, and looks down at the floor in sadness.)

Well, you three seem to having fun. I guess you don't need me for that any more.

ALEXANDER:
(He speaks with total sincerity and with real feeling.)

OF COURSE, I need you; you're the other part of me.

HEPHAISTON:
(Now he raises his head. Looking now right at Alexander, he almost shouts and he raises his hands, making fists.)

Is that MAKE UP on your face?   Has this sissy boy turned you into him?
(He shakes his head in disbelief and horror.)
What have you BECOME? I don't even know you anymore.

ALEXANDER:
(He looks and sounds full of deep concern for Hephaiston.)

I'm still ME;   I'm still your best friend;   you've known me all your life; I'm still the man you LOVE.

HEPHAISTON:
(He looks confused,conflicted, unsure so he talks in a softer voice than usual.)

I'm not sure any more. I HOPE so.

(His voice gets stronger now in an attempt to get back to normal business.)

You'd better come with me now. Your generals, the men you've known since we were boys together--- they're starting to drink without us.

ALEXANDER:
Sisygambis, dear mother and great queen, I have to leave you now to go to a men's event. I hope you have sweet dreams tonight.
(He kisses her on both cheeks. She gets up and starts to leave but turns back to say one thing to him, and then she leaves without expecting a response.)

SISYGAMBIS:
Please be careful, Alexander. I have a bad feeling about tonight.

HEPHAISTON:
(He puts his hand on Alexander, trying to get him going.)
We really have to go. I can hear them drinking already. I'm ready for a drink, that's for sure.

ALEXANDER:
(He puts his arm around Hephaiston and they start to move, then he remembers Persian Boy so he turns his head back to talk to him.)

Me too!
Sweet boy, come with us. You're part of our team now.

HEPHAISTON:
(He suddenly looks very angry, and he pulls away from Alexander.)

The HELL he is. That silly "girl" is NO part of me.
(He walks away fast and says as he leaves....)
I'm going to drink with our old friends; you do as you choose.

ALEXANDER:
(He puts his arm around Persian Boy and pulls him towards the party area. Persian Boy looks reluctant to go.)

You're coming with me now. I'll show them who's king here.

Teacher please say, "Now I need the following characters standing in a group: PARMENION, PTOLEMY, BLACK CLEITUS, WHITE CHEITUS, and HARPALOS."

FIRST NARRATOR:

On one side of the stage are Alexander's generals: Parmenion who is the top general and the only old man there, Ptolemy, Black Cleitus, (named for his very dark hair) White Cleitus, and Harpalos. All are standing up, talking loudly, and drinking often from their wine beakers. At first they don't notice Hephaiston as he comes in. Hephaiston stands several feet back from them. When Alexander and Persian Boy come in, Hephaiston keeps several feet away from them too, as if he's physically showing his separation from both groups.

BLACK CLEITUS:

(From his words and body language it's obvious that he's already had a lot to drink, the others not so much.)

Why don't we bring it out in the open? You think about it, and I do too. I'll say it out loud: IS ALEXANDER GOING PERSIAN ON US?

PTOLOMY:

I don't think it's appropriate for us to talk about. He's the King of Macedonia and of Greece, and he's the best general in the world. Who are we to question anything he does?

HARPALOS:

And he's been our FRIEND since we were all in the royal school together. I'm loyal to my friends all the time.

WHITE CLEITUS:

Me too. Besides, he's made us rich! After every battle, he shares the valuable things we win. This time he gave me a TALENT of gold--- that's a big pile of gold!

PARMENION:

Yes, he's generous and yes, he's great, but now he's doing things his father Philip NEVER would do. He associates with Persians more and more. He talks their barbarian language too.

BLACK CLEITUS:
(He frowns deeply and nearly shouts.)

He fucking SLEEPS with them! Here he comes now with his arm around that nelly boy of his. He ought to be ashamed.

PTOLEMY:
Keep your voices down, will you? Now, Hephaiston, how do you feel about this? You're his best friend after all.

HEPHAISTON:

He says it's business really. He says he gets ideas from the boy, things that help him make decisions better.

BLACK CLEITUS:
(He practically SHOUTS.)

We all know what he gets from that sissy boy!

SECOND NARRATOR:
Alexander comes up near Black Cleitus, about five feet away from him. The Persian Boy stays right beside his king. Alexander's face turns red as he explodes in anger, and shakes his fist at Black Cleitus.

ALEXANDER:

I HEARD THAT, you fool! How DARE you criticize my friend. You take that back or DIE!

FIRST NARRATOR:

Alexander gets so mad that he puts himself into a sort of epileptic seizure, an altered state where he seems to loose connection to the world. His eyes close but he still stands up, motionless and blank-faced.

BLACK CLEITUS:
(He now totally lost in drunken rage. He pulls out a hidden knife from his clothes and moves fast to Alexander, trying to kill him.)

No, YOU die, Alexander!

FIRST NARRATOR:

In a flash, the Persian Boy puts himself in front of Alexander,and so the Persian Boy takes the blow meant for the King. The knife goes into his chest, making him fall immediately to the floor. He lays there lifeless.
    Alexander stands still, with his eyes closed. Hephaiston gets out his knife and stabs Black Cleitus in the heart. He dies almost immediately.

SECOND NARRATOR:

Hephaiston sees that Alexander is untouched, so he turns to the Persian Boy; he kneels down and takes the Persian Boy's head onto his lap. From the limpness of his neck, it's obvious the boy is dead. Alexander still is "absent", lost in shock. His face looks blank,and his eyes are still shut.

HEPHAISTON:

 You saved his life, you SAVED his life. *(He kisses Persian Boy several times on check.)* I can't believe you did it--- and not me.
He was so close to death, and I did NOTHING. You saved him for us all.
    And I always hated you. I thought you weren't a man; we all did.

We called you sissy boy. But you proved us wrong. What's a man but courage and competence? You showed both just now. You're more a man than any of us.

FIRST NARRATOR:

Alexander suddenly leaves his altered state. He opens his eyes, blinking several times. He looks around in amazement, then he looks down to see the two dead bodies.

ALEXANDER:

What's going on? What's happened to my boy?

HEPHAISTON:
(He takes Alexander into his arms to comfort him. Alexander starts to cry and sob. Of course so does Hephaiston.)

He took a blow that was meant for you. Black Cleitus tried to kill you with a knife. Your boy moved fast to take the blow. He saved your life. He's a HERO, true.

ALEXANDER:

I can't believe he gave his life for me.
He's my hero too.
People said he wasn't really a man,
But then he proved them wrong
Now that his short life is gone,.
What I do next must be his burial song.

SCENE TEN------------------ **" THE INCLUSIVE WEDDING"**

MAY 1, 333 B.C.

CHARACTERS:
*(Parts marked with a * have no speaking parts.)*

NARRATOR
ALEXANDER
HEPHAISTON
QUEEN SISYGOMBIS
FOURTH SOLDIER *
FIFTH SOLDIER *
THE STALLION *
HECTOR, HIS BOY *
FIRST MOUNTAIN WOMAN *
SECOND MOUNTAIN WOMAN *
CHASE, THEIR SON *
LYDIA *
LIONGUARD *
PRINCESS ANN *
KRISTY, HER GIRLFRIEND *
TRANSGENDERED PRIEST *
HIS BEAR BOYFRIEND *
PARMENION *
PTOLEMY *
HARPALOS *
WHITE CLEITUS *
SIX ROYAL GIRLS *

NARRATOR:

It's a week after the Persian Boy was killed. The inclusive wedding that was his dream will start in a few minutes. All the characters are in their most beautiful clothes: shinning armor, silks in rainbow hues, jewels flashing everywhere.

They're gathered in the largest indoor space in the world. The interior is entirely made of gleaming snow-white marble, with richly colored Persian carpets on the floor. Magnificent fountains of gold shoot perfumed water in the air.

At one end of the hall there's a raised platform made of silver inlaid with countless diamonds. In the center of it is a canopy of sky blue silk hanging from tall pillars of rock crystal. Under the canopy, dressed entirely in silver cloth and diamond jewels, stands Sisygambis, now called QUEEN MOTHER OF THE WORLD. With her are her six granddaughters, dressed in royal purple.

Thousands of guests pack the room, standing on either side of an aisle. They all have silver baskets of roses petals, ready to throw. In the background is heard the music of a hundred harps played by people barely visible behind pink silk curtains.

Teacher, please say: " I need all the following characters up in front. These people are in line, waiting to walk down the aisle. Fourth Soldier and Fifth Soldier(from Scene One,) both big,hairy men with their arms around each other; The Stallion of the Leathermen Army and his young Hector(from Scene Two), both in black leather; Lydia and Lionguard of the Lesbian Legion, both wearing lion skins and armor(from Scene Three); First Mountain Woman and Second Mountain Woman(from Scene Five),wearing simple but dignified dresses,and their handsome son; the Princess Ann,(from Scene Six) wearing subtle make up and lipstick, talking to Princess Christy a pretty, smart-looking woman with her; the Transgendered Priest(from Scene Six) with a masculine older man who obviously likes him a lot.

Nearby but clearly in a group of their own are Ptolemy, Parmenion, White Cleitus, and Harpalos, all Alexander's generals.

A little off by themselves, the Great Alexander and his Hephaiston are deep in conversation, giving their full attention to each other as usual.

At the other end of the room stand Queen Mother Sisygambis and her six granddaughters, the Royal Girls."

******* (Since so many people are involved in this scene, it might be best to not have the characters come up, but rather have them read from their seats.}

ALEXANDER:

I'm glad we decided to go on with this. At first I thought we had to cancel because he died, but now I'm glad we're going to do it.

HEPHAISTON:

(He uses his arm in a swiping way to mean "just look at all this".)
He'd be so PROUD! This was his idea, and look at how it's all turned out.

ALEXANDER:

Most of all, he'd be proud of YOU--- of how you've grown in tolerance. A month ago you hated diversity--- in race and in sexuality both. Now you embrace it. His death taught you so much.

HEPHAISTON:

It did for sure. I'm just sorry he had to die for me to learn. I could have learned so much from him alive.

ALEXANDER:

This inclusive wedding will be his final message to us all. Let's get it started now.

(In a loud voice he says....)

MUSICIANS, begin the WEDDING MARCH at once.

NARRATOR:

A large band of trumpets and other horns comes out from behind the silk curtains. They play appropriate brass music. Alexander now addresses the assembled members of the wedding. When he talks to each couple, they bow low to him. Then that couple begins to slowly walk down the aisle, while a thousand people on the aisle throw rose petals in the air. The spectators who are further back start to applaud loudly when each new couple begins the wedding walk.

ALEXANDER:

My big, brave soldiers, first I want you to go down the aisle. Your manly strength was the foundation for our victory!

(Fourth and Fifth Soldiers join hands and then go down the aisle. The crowd throws rose petals and claps loudly.)

You Leathermen are next. I want the Stallion and his boy now to go down the aisle. Your fine horsemanship helped us win the prize!

(They join hands and then go down the aisle.   The crowd throws rose petals and claps loudly.)

Next the Lesbian Legion represented by their new Queen Lydia and Lionguard. Your speed and skill saved the day for us!

(Same--join hands, down the aisle with petals and clapping.)

Now I want the mountain women and their son, that strong and faithful family,who showed me the hidden pass that was the secret to our success!

(Same)

Next the Princess Ann and Princess Christy, two fine women who make more beauty and art wherever they go.
(Same)

Next I want the Transgendered Priest and the man we just found for him.   Your determination to be yourself is a lesson to us all.
(Same)

Last of all I call my highest ranking officers, the generals of my army. Without your leadership, I'd have no army at all. I know you men aren't eager to marry foreign girls, but wait until you see the ones we have for you. There they are up on the platform, as beautiful as can be, and with them go their fathers' lands so you will be great Persian lords. My mighty men, now march down the aisle.
(Same)

NARRATOR:

When all the couples have come down the aisle, they line up near Queen Mother Sisygambis. Then each couple comes up to the Queen Mother and kneels before her. She takes one hand from each person and holds it as she says this once to each couple:

QUEEN SISYGAMBIS:

We accept you as you are.
We support your search for love.
We welcome you to our new, inclusive world!

NARRATOR:

When each couple is married like this, they go back to where they'd been standing. Now she looks at the four generals, beckoning them to come up to her. She then goes to the royal girls, and one by one she leads a girl to a general, who takes her hand. When she's done with that, she says loudly to the whole assembly.

SISYGAMBIS:

Great generals of Greece, I now join you to these royal girls and to their lands. May you produce together a new race that will value the individual and cherish the group as well. May you become our better future!

NARRATOR:

Suddenly the sound of a very large drum is heard. Four times it booms with long pauses in between. The spotlight of attention goes to Alexander and Hephaiston who are still standing back where the rest had been.

Alexander and Hephaiston each put an arm around the other's waist, and begin a slow walk side by side down the aisle. The drum sounds for each step they take, until they reach the front. The audience is stone silent and motionless. Every eye is on them.

When they reach the platform, each of them goes up to one of Sisygambis's granddaughters and takes her hand.

Alexander and Hephaiston then face the crowd. Each puts one arm around the other's shoulder. Alexander and Hephaiston say together in a loud voice....

ALEXANDER and HEPHAISTON:
It's our turn now; we must practice what we preach.
We'll take these wives so we can teach.

ALEXANDER:
"Our love will conquer time", I've often said.
I now know how! Your children and mine will grow up together,
half Persian, half Greek.
They'll combine the best of both worlds, and build the peace
we seek.

HEPHAISTON:
Their children will marry other people too, of different colors and
dreams.
They'll make a new rainbow people , the most beautiful ever seen.

*(They both are getting more and more excited by their dreams. They GLOW
with hope and with love for each other.)*

ALEXANDER:

This new race will will be different, inside and out.
They'll value the INDIVIDUAL, but they'll care about the GROUP too.
They'll live by both values, in everything they do!

ALEXANDER and HEPHAISTON together:
(Alexander takes one of Hephaiston's hands in one of his.)

If this is going to happen, we must begin it TODAY!
Take the hands of the people around you---that's what we say.

*(All the people in the audience should now STAND UP and TAKE THE
HAND of a person standing near them.)*

Tolerance and love start HERE today.
Now that we've learned it's the very best way!
And we've learned it----in this PLAY!

RIGHT AS THE PLAY ENDS THE TEACHER SHOULD PERHAPS PLAY ANDREW LLOYD WEBER'S "LOVE CHANGES EVERYTHING". I used this song at the end with a somewhat similar play once and it went well. We paraded out of the room, still holding hands, with a portable music player. It felt really good! You might want to try this.

ASSESSMENTS FOR QA

First assignment

"YOU AS A PERSON IN THE PLAY "

PLEASE PICK ONE CHARACTER IN THE PLAY. GET TOTALLY INSIDE THAT CHARACTER; IMAGINE YOU ARE THAT PERSON. NOW INVENT WHAT YOU THINK YOUR CHARACTER WOULD ANSWER TO EACH OF THESE VERY PERSONAL QUESTIONS. YOU WILL HAVE TO INVENT MANY OF THESE THINGS SINCE SOME WILL NOT BE IN THE PLAY. BE CREATIVE, BUT KEEP IN MIND THE TIME AND PLACE YOU ARE SUPPOSED TO BE IN. PLEASE PUT EACH ANSWER ON A SEPARATE LINE, AS IN THE EXAMPLE GIVEN BELOW. PLEASE READ THE EXAMPLE BELOW NOW, MY POEM CALLED "BIG BEAR".

Who are you?
How old are you?
What do you look like?
What do you do for a living?
What's one specific thing you do when you're on the job?
What is another example of what you do on your job, and how well do you do it?
What do you like to do when you have sex? Anything else?
What do you think is a good thing about your sexual (style) (type)?(or What is a good thing about you as a sexual person?)
What is a negative about it, if there is some thing?
When you think about your past, what specific memories
 come to mind?
What concerns/worries you at this present time of your life?
What would you really like to happen to you in your future?
Do you think this is probably going to happen to you in your future?
Why do you think that?

EXAMPLE POEM

BIG BEAR

by Mickey Welch

I'm a bear I guess, a soldier in Alexander's army.
I'm forty but I look older , and I feel it in my bones.
My beard's half gray ,and I'm getting bald.
I'm in the infantry--Second Regiment, Fifth Brigade.
I guess I mostly march,
But in a battle I use my sword to kill.
I do it damned well, I'd say;
Last time I got five men in a day.
In sex, I used to like to fuck my old wife,
But now I like to do it to my buddy better.
Something bad about me is that I'll have no more sons, but I've already got three, so
that's enough for me.
The thing I remember most is when my boys hung on to me when I said goodbye.
That made me cry.
I worry about getting hurt bad, loosing an arm or leg.
A one-armed man's not worth a lot, is he?
In the future, I'd like to shake hands with Alexander, with our hero-king.
My friend here did. He said Alexander sort of glowed, like the sun.
I'd like to see that too.
He loves his men I've heard. He'll get around soon to meet us all.
That's the kind of man he is.
That's why I'd die for him.

_____

Second assignment

" HAVE YOU EVER NOTICED THAT SOME PEOPLE CHANGE A LOT IN A SHORT TIME?"

Please think of the main characters in "QUEERING ALEXANDER" in terms of their
changes. Now write a paragraph in which you tell us what character you think changes
the most. Tell us what the person was like before and then after the change. Use
specific things from the play to show what you mean. End your paragraph with your
answer to this: WAS THE CHANGE MORE GOOD OR MORE BAD? WHY?

Now please do the same thing with another character in the Welch play who changes
quite a bit. Again tell us what that person is like before and then after the change. As

before, use examples from the play to show what you mean. Please end this paragraph by answering: WAS THE CHANGE MORE GOOD OR MORE in your opinion and WHY do you say that?

If you choose to, please write a third paragraph about YOURSELF. Did any thing in the play cause you to think or feel differently than you did before? Do you think this change was more good or more bad for you? Why? Do you think other people could be helped by this play? Why?

TEST ON "QUEERING ALEXANDER"

1. In the year 333 b.c., Alexander is the king of what country?
a. Macedonia (Macedon) b. Athens c. Sparta
_____

2. At that time, what empire was the traditional enemy of Alexander's country?
a. the Roman Empire b. the Persian Empire c. the Chinese Empire
_____

3. As the play begins, which side is richer and has a much larger army?
a. Alexander's side   b. the Persian Empire   c. Rome
_____

4. Why is the Sacred Band of Thebes famous?
a. because only it won a battle against Alexander
b. because it was made up only of gay partners and because they fought until the last man died

_____

5. How was homosexuality sometimes dealt with in education among the upper class men of ancient Athens?
a. An older man would match up with a younger one with similar interests. The older one would teach the younger one to excel at their shared interest.
b. It was totally forbidden. If anyone was found out to be gay, that person was expelled from school immediately.

_____

6. In the play, why do the two soldiers decide they have to try to kill Alexander?

a. because he is gay and they hate gays in the military
b. because he will keep the army fighting so long that the soldiers will probably be killed

_____

7. Who is Alexander's life-partner?
a. Hephaiston   b. Ptolemy   c. Black Cleitus
_____

8. What do these partners say is one of the main
reasons for their success in their relationship?
a. They look alike.   b. They're the same age.   c. They
have a commitment to kindness

_____

9. Why does Hephaiston get mad at Alexander in Scene
Two?
a. because Alexander has sex with the Persian Boy
b. because Alexander is too close to his bossy mother
_____

10.   In the play, how do the Leathermen of Thrace
fight?
a. on foot, using sling shots
b. on elephants, using poison arrows
c. on chariots, with one guy driving and another guy
fighting
_____

11. According to one character in the play, what is the
brotherhood of Leathermen based on?
a. on the love of power and male aggressiveness
b. on being a good Christian
_____

12.   When Hector says he's called a loser, what does
his friend Jason say?
a. "They're right.   You are a wallflower.   Why don't
you man up?"
b. "You're a real man, that's for sure, but maybe your
style of manhood would fit in better some place else.

_____

13. What are two reasons everyone but Alexander hates the Persian Boy?
a. because he is "feminine"(like Curt in "Glee") and because he is Persian
b. because they say he is ugly and also as dumb as a doornail

_____

14. How does Alexander plan on using the Leathermen of Thrace in the coming battle?
a. He'll use them as foot soldiers and have them run at the Persians.
b. He'll use them as a mobile force to surprise the Persians.

_____

15. Why do One Eye and his friends try to hurt the two mountain women and their boy Chase?
a. because they think the mountain women are on the Persian side and they hate Persians
b. because One Eye says, "Two women-lovers and a kid do NOT make a real family!"

_____

16. What does Alexander learn from their boy Chase?

a. He learns that right now there is an open pass through the mountains so Alexander can get people behind the Persians

b. He learns that the Persians are coming up into the mountains to conquer the women's area.

_____

17. In this play, there is a transgendered person. What does this person do for a living?

a. She/he is a circus performer and a singer for parties.
b. She/he is a priest in the worship of the goddess Cybele.

18. Which of the following sentences describe the Royal Twin, the sister of the Persian King Darius?
a. "She's not bi like me---she's a total lesbian, even if she does look and act like a traditional woman. She's very feminine, lipstick and all."
b. "She looks just like a man---pants and all."

19. Why does her mother, Queen Mother Sisygambis, decide to go along with Royal Twin's idea to kill her brother?

a. because she black mails her mother, threatening to tell a terrible secret.
b. because Queen Sisygambis realizes that her daughter, Royal Twin, could save the Persian Empire from Alexander, but her son, King Darius is too weak to save it.

20. In this play, how did the Lesbian Legion get started?
a. The Persian King needed a new group for his army so he started this legion to ride his elephants. Elephants like the sound of women's voices so this worked out well.

b. The Greek poet Sappho attracted young women to her home island by her fame. A sort of women's college got started there. Its graduates needed a job so they started the Lesbian Legion to make a living without men.

21. In this play, why does Alexander's side win the big battle against the Persians?
a. because Alexander's men have invented a new kind of siege weapon that hurls hundreds of arrows at one time.

b. because the Lesbian Legion has used Chase's way through the mountains to get behind the Persians so they surprise the Persians and use their dead-eye accurate arrows to scare the Persians into running away. Women Warriors Rule!

_____

22. After the battle, how does the Queen Mother Sisygambis start to feel about Alexander?
a. She feels that he is a much better man than her son was so she loves him as her new son.
b. She hates him because he has killed so many of her Persian people and has disgraced her son.

_____

23. What new idea does Alexander come up with after the big battle?
a. He now wants to wipe out all the Persians and give their land to the Jews.
b. He wants to bring the Greeks and the Persians together to make a new, more tolerant people.

_____

24. What does the Persian Boy suggest be added to Alexander's wedding idea?
a. He wants to include Jews and Buddhists in the wedding.
b. He wants to also include bears, leathermen, lipstick lesbians,etc. in the wedding.

_____

25. In the play, when the Persian Boy dies to save Alexander, how does Hephaiston react?
a. He now realizes that the Persian Boy is a real man and a real hero.
b. He's glad his rival is finally gone.